READ
ABOUT
me©

Miller®

Black Texans

They Overcame

Black Texans

They Overcame

By Marian E. Barnes

EAKIN PRESS ⬗ Austin, TX

Library of Congress Cataloging-in-Publication Data

Barnes, Marian E.
    Black Texans who overcame / by Marian E. Barnes.
        p.   cm.
    Includes bibliographical references (p.   ) and index.
    ISBN 1-57168-055-1
    1. Afro-Americans — Texas — Biography — Juvenile literature. 2. Texas —
Biography — Juvenile literature. I. Title.
E185.96.B29   1996
976.4'00496073'00922--dc20
[B]   95-30229
                                                                                              CIP
                                                                                              AC

For my granddaughters

Alexandra Katherine "Katie" Stewart
and
Victoria Danielle "'Toria" Stewart

and the new sweet baby

with love

and a prayer for you and your generation:

"May you discover the deepest depths of your inner being,
learn who you are, and reach for the highest, brightest star
in the universe to make it your contribution to the world!"

Contents

Acknowledgments

Many people and institutions helped me compile the stories in this collection. However, this book would not have become a reality without the contributions of those named below. With sincere thanks and gratitude, I acknowledge their help. In Austin, Texas: Ada Anderson, director of the Leadership-Educational-Arts-Program (LEAP); Melissa Derkacz, Edwin and Charlene Eakin, and Melissa Roberts of Eakin Press; Clifton Griffin, branch manager, Carver Library; Dr. Beulah Agnes Curry Jones, chairwoman, Music Department, Huston-Tillotson College; Dr. Marvin Kimbrough, chairwoman, Division of Humanities, Huston-Tillotson College; Robert Mayott, library clerk, University Hills Library; Deborah Orr-Ogunro, director, Outreach Productions; Bernadette Pfifer, curator, Carver Museum; Jesse Mercer, Fuller-Sheffield Funeral Services; Frank Schmitzer, branch manager, University Hills Library; James and Joan Stewart, editorial assistance and moral support; Henry Washington, assistant professor of music/choral director, Huston-Tillotson College; Austin History Center; Austin Public Library; and University of Texas libraries and archives.

Also, Charlese James, Fort Worth Arts Council, Fort Worth, Texas; Sarah Trotty, chairwoman, Fine Arts Department, Texas Southern University, Houston, Texas; and Vivian Ayers, curator of the Adept New American Museum, Mt. Vernon, New York.

PLEASE NOTE

In this collection, when referring to race, the word "Black" is a proper noun which identifies the *race and culture* of African-Americans who vary in skin color from ebony-black to pearl-white. The word "white," on the other hand, is an adjective which describes the approximate *skin color* of European races and nations (French, Italian, or Norwegian, for example).

"Black," meaning race or culture, is the counterpart of such words as "Irish," "German," "French," and "English," which identify the race or culture of people from countries in Europe.

In addition, like the word "Asian," which relates to things, people or countries on the continent of Asia, and the word "European," which relates to things, people or countries on the continent of Europe, the words "African" and "Black" relate to things, people, and countries on the continent of Africa.

Debbie Allen

Superstar in the Entertainment Industry

When DEBBIE ALLEN was in high school, her classmates named her "Miss Versatility," and now the world knows why. The gifted entertainer sings, dances, and acts for the eye of a camera or on stage for an audience. On the other hand, almost as often as she is in the spotlight, she is the writer, director, choreographer, or producer behind the scenes on stage, television, and film.

Her work has been outstanding in all of these areas, earning more awards than can be listed. Television audiences around the world adored her as the dance teacher "Lydia Grant" on the prime-time TV hit *FAME*. But most viewers did not know Debbie Allen was behind the camera directing many of the shows, or that she was choreographer-director for the series. Her work on *FAME* earned her two EMMY awards for choreographing and directing the dance scenes, and a Golden Globe Award as "Best Actress in a TV Series."

"I love to be able to go from acting to directing," Debbie said. "I'm fickle. Whatever I'm doing at the moment is the thing I like best. When I was performing in *Sweet Charity,* there was no where else I wanted to be. I need to perform. But lately I think there is nothing quite as exciting as directing. In essence, you're designing the whole show. When you get it right, there's nothing better. But it's also the most tiring job, and I wouldn't want to be doing it all the time. I'm a passionate woman, and I'm moved to work because it makes me feel so good. If I didn't love my work, I wouldn't have the energy to do all the things I've done. But my work is a discipline, a way of life."[1]

"This lady is stretched to the absolute limit and it doesn't show," Mel Swope, producer of the *FAME* TV series said of

!Debbie Allen. Because of her ability to be superior in so many different areas, Swope described her as "a genius."[2]

Debbie directed the final episode in the *FAME* series. "The final show was special," she observed. "It was something like a reunion with a lot of the old kids coming back. I worked with a wonderful group of people, and I'm sure I'll miss them. I learned so much on the show, but I really feel it's time to try my wings."[3]

"Actually, there's hardly a time when she's not trying her wings," her sister, Phylicia Rashad, commented, "and they're usually flapping in four directions at once. Debbie has tremendous energy, unlike anything I've ever seen. Debbie's in this little body, but she has always chosen to do things that were much bigger than that little body. And she doesn't let anything stop her."[4]

Debbie Allen was born in Houston, Texas, January 16, 1950, to Andrew Allen, a dentist, now deceased, and Vivian Ayers Allen. Her mother, who uses the name Vivian Ayers, is a poet and an author. Her book of poetry entitled *Spice of Dawn* was nominated for a Pulitzer Prize. Debbie's sister, Phylicia Rashad, is also a multi-talented entertainer. She became one of America's best known actresses as the TV wife of comedian Bill Cosby on *The Cosby Show*. Andrew "Tex" Allen, brother of Phylicia and Debbie, is a noted composer of jazz as well as a skilled trumpeter and pianist.

Debbie grew up at a time when racial prejudice was a way of life in the South. For African-Americans, many theaters and schools were "off limits," and Debbie was not free to develop her talents in any school of her choice. But Houston was wonderful in other ways for the little girl.

"Growing up in a place where you could see the sun, the sky, and have a lot of trees and grass, you felt like you really had a place in this universe," she said.[5]

When Debbie was little more than a toddler, her father and mother separated. However, both parents continued to show their children interest and love. Their dad, who lived close by, spent time with his children or phoned them every day. He was "a fun dad," always laughing and joking, and playing games with them. But the minute their grades

Debbie Allen

weren't good, he saw to it that the fun and games took a back seat until their grades improved.

Debbie began taking dance lessons when she was three years old. Her mother believed Debbie had a special gift for dancing. Sometimes she would say Debbie had been born to dance. When she was eight years old, her mother tried to enroll her in the Houston Foundation for Ballet. However, the Foundation appeared to have a policy of racial segregation, and Debbie was not accepted. Vivian Ayers remained determined. She arranged for Debbie to take private lessons from a ballet star instead.

One day when Debbie was eleven, her mom walked into the house and told the children they were moving to Mexico City. They had never been out of the country before. It was an exciting time! Living in Mexico was an adventure that sharpened their minds and caused them to look at life in a different way.

Debbie learned a great deal about the Mexican people and their culture. She also learned to speak Spanish very well. In addition, she was able to study at the Ballet Nacional de Mexico and attend performances of the Ballet Folklorico de Mexico.

In spite of her obvious talent, success did not come easily or quickly to Debbie Allen. Shortly before she graduated from high school, she auditioned for the dance program at North Carolina School of the Arts, the college she hoped to attend. Debbie's audition was excellent. She danced so well she was asked to give a demonstration for others who were auditioning. Then, to her surprise, she was denied admission.

Her sister was furious. "They told her she did not have the body of a dancer, that she would never be a dancer," Phylicia said. "She was so talented, and here was this *cock-eyed* person telling her to forget it! Deborah was so hurt that she did not dance for one year. And dancing had always been her life."[6]

Crushed by the rejection, Debbie did stop dancing. She enrolled at Howard University, where she became an honor student. Then Mike Malone, Howard University's dance choreographer, encouraged her to begin dancing again.

In the end, finding the strength to keep going in the face

4

of rejection paid off. Debbie not only became one of the world's most respected dancers, she also was awarded an honorary doctor's degree by North Carolina School of the Arts, the school that had refused to enroll her as a dance student. In addition, she received an honorary doctorate from Howard University.

Actually, when she was quite young, Debbie set a pattern of struggling for whatever she wanted and refusing to give up no matter what happened. Phylicia enjoys remembering the time Debbie competed in a school swimming race:

"Deborah came in last but she never stopped swimming. She swam and swam. The race had been over for five minutes, and she was still swimming! She wasn't gonna win the race, but she was gonna finish it. And when she did finish, the poor child had to be dragged out of the water by the vice-principal. Everybody was cheering — I think they cheered more for her than they did for the winner — because she kept going. And Debbie has always been like that."[7]

The sisters are extremely happy in their professional lives, their personal lives, and in their love for each other. Debbie is quick to give credit to Phylicia for helping her to become successful. "Everything I've done, Phylicia helped me to do," she said. "We were very close growing up, and I guess we've gotten even closer as we got older."[8] She further explained:

"I'm so happy about our successes, our good fortune and our relationship. Phylicia is my best friend and a terrific big sister. We speak to each other at least once a week, more than that if there's a lot of gossip. We don't discuss our careers that much, but we do keep each other up to date on what's happening. Mostly we talk about our personal lives — how we're feeling about things, what's happening with our husbands, and with our children. They are what matter most."[9]

Debbie and Phylicia lead lives that are alike in many ways. Both are singers, dancers, and actresses. Both were graduated with honors from Howard University. And together they have established a $10,000 scholarship in memory of their father, Dr. Andrew Allen. The scholarship is awarded through the Drama Department of Howard University to a versatile college senior student who excels in acting, singing, and dancing.

Both sisters married young, divorced, and remarried sports celebrities. Phylicia is the wife of Ahmad Rashad, a former football hero who became a sports announcer. They live in New York and have one daughter, Condola Phylea. Phylicia also has a son, Billy, from a former marriage. Debbie is married to basketball star Norman Nixon. They live in Los Angeles and have one son, Norman, Jr., and one daughter, Vivian Nichole. She was named for Vivian Ayers, Debbie's mother.

"We think Vivian is following in my footsteps," Debbie said when her daughter was three years old. "She loves to dance, and we're always dancing around together. She listens to all kinds of music, from Janet Jackson to *Porgy and Bess*, and really goes crazy over *Carmen Jones*, especially the song 'Beat Out Dat Rhythm on a Drum.' She also likes basketball games and sometimes sits on the bench with Norm, but so far she hasn't picked up a basketball."[10]

Debbie Allen praises her mother for providing guidance and sharing knowledge and wisdom that helped her, Phylicia, and Andrew to become successful and achieve happiness.[11] The eyes of the energetic artist light up, and her voice rings with enthusiasm as she describes her mom: "My mother's an artist. She's a writer, she's painted and she could have been a concert pianist. She is a genuine scholar. She ran a museum in Texas for years. It would be hard to grow up in a house with a woman like that and not develop some talent. When we were five, we were studying music and dance at a local school, and then we went after whatever interested us."[12]

Debbie thinks it's important to study. She believes young people should study themselves, learn who they really are, and prepare for their life's work. "If you can look in the mirror and know who you are and what's going on, you're on your way. Many times people are held back because they're not ready artistically or mentally, or they're going through some kind of trauma in their personal lives that they're not strong enough to overcome," she has said.[13]

Explaining the success she and Phylicia achieved, she added, "There are so many factors involved in success. Any moments of hesitation we might have had or any setbacks we might have encountered were offset by the fact that we believed in ourselves. We never lost sight of that goal, that dream of being successful in whatever we were trying to do."[14]

But in what seems to be her "bottom line" on achieving success, she harks to her Texas roots. "Maybe we have a different attitude coming from Texas," she said. "I mean, we don't do any of that lost souls trying to find ourselves routine. Child, that wouldn't go down in Texas. We hustle, hustle all the time!"[15]

Vivian Ayers

Mother, Poet, Author, Museum Curator

VIVIAN AYERS looked lovely. Flawless, caramel-colored skin, soft, waving, silvery hair in which a trace of black still lingered, sensitive eyes with a jewel-like sparkle. She stood in the center of an eager group of women quietly autographing the books some offered.

"*Ooooooooooh,* let me touch you," one young woman said. "Maybe something will rub off on me." She laughed and leaned her shoulder against the shoulder of Vivian Ayers. Others laughed and moved forward wanting to touch her too. They could have been mistaken for a group of happy school girls. They were not.

These were women attending awards ceremonies in honor of achievers cited in a new book, *Black Texas Women.*[1] Some of them were featured in the book just as Vivian Ayers had been. Many well-known celebrities were present, including Lady Bird Johnson, widow of former U.S. President Lyndon Baines Johnson, and their daughter, Luci Baines Johnson.

What was there about Vivian Ayers that made her stand out even among this group of women being honored for superior achievements? What did these women see in her character that made them want to be more like her?

Vivian Ayers had done many things to be admired. To

7

begin with, she had managed to stay young. It was hard to believe she was over seventy because she looked and acted little more than half her age. Her book of poems, *Spice of Dawn*, was nominated for a Pulitzer Prize in the 1950s. However, she is much more than a poet. Her daughter, Debbie Allen, once described her mother as a writer, artist, painter, and scholar who ran a museum in Texas for years, and played a piano so well she could have been a concert pianist.[2] But the world spotlight may shine on Vivian Ayers most of all for her success at a job many people take for granted. She is frequently singled out and praised for being a good mother, especially for helping to develop the talents of her offspring.

Three of her children became famous entertainers: Andrew "Tex" Allen, a jazz composer and musician, plays the trumpet, and, like his mother, is a pianist. He wrote the music for one of her poems for a pre-Mother's Day TV show in 1988. Award-winning Debbie Allen is a dancer, a choreographer, a singer, and an actress. She is also a director, a writer, and a producer. In addition, Debbie has composed music. Phylicia Rashad, Vivian Ayers' eldest daughter, is a talented singer, dancer, and actress. Her role as Claire Huxtable, the TV wife of Bill Cosby on *The Cosby Show,* made her one of the most famous women in the world.

For Vivian Ayers, being a mother meant loving her children as their teacher, guidance counselor, and friend. She studied each of her children carefully so she would know how to satisfy that child's special needs. Once, she moved with her young daughters to Mexico. There both girls learned to speak Spanish, attended ballet performances by famous Mexican dancers, and took dancing lessons at the Ballet Nacional de Mexico.

After her children were adults, someone asked her what she had taught them when they were growing up. "I told them what I tell them now," she said, ". . . always seek new knowledge. . . . There must always be some kind of program, some new study, some challenge to jack the mind up and make it use some of the cells it hasn't used before."[3]

What do her children think of her as a person, and as a mother? "Phenomenal," is what they say of her. They also say she is "ahead of her time."[4]

Vivian Ayers

Vivian Ayers lived in Houston, Texas, for nearly forty years. Her children were born there — Phylicia in 1948, and Debbie in 1950. She was married to Dr. Andrew Allen, a dentist. She and her husband separated when the children were young, but he remained a caring, loving father until his death in 1984. When her daughters reached college age they enrolled at Howard University in Washington, DC. Both graduated with honors and moved to New York to pursue their careers.

By 1988, the careers of the children were going well. Debbie was living in Los Angeles, Phylicia was in New York, and so was Andrew. One day the phone rang. "They (Phylicia and Debbie) called and asked me if I wanted to live in the house Debbie bought back in the seventies," the beautiful mother remembered. "The allure of not having to ever pay rent again made me say yes."[5]

The spacious home into which she moved was in Mt. Vernon, New York, not far from the homes of Phylicia and Andrew. In addition to providing her a house, her daughters offered to finance a museum similar to the Adept Museum she had established in Houston in 1970. A Greek scholar, Vivian said she selected the name "Adept" because it means "free and unmastered" in Greek.

Vivian Ayers turned the first floor of her new home into the Adept New American Museum, which displays the art and culture of the Southwest. "I started Adept to communicate the history of the American Southwest through poetry, visual arts, music, and dance," she explained. Items in the museum were acquired through a lifetime of collecting. Paintings and prints by famous artists decorate the walls. Huge drapes of African and Aztec fabrics cascade from the ceiling. Mayan ceramics line the fireplace. Pottery and one-of-a-kind pieces fill shelves and tables.

One corner is dedicated to the lives and careers of African-American astronauts. Another corner has pictures that tell the story of cowboys of all races. Adept's most popular work, titled "Hello, Goya," is in a separate area. Acquired in the early 1980s, it is a sculpture of a bull made of recycled wire and metal by artist Jesse Lott. The striking creation draws all eyes to it. Even today, after so many years, the museum curator says of the sculpture, "It just won't let go of me."[6]

Works in the museum were chosen to teach and expand the knowledge of visitors, especially about Black heritage and history. Vivian Ayers explains, "We are proud and thriving Americans, yet we remain ignorant of many things which are essential to our culture and to our command of destiny."

People in the Mt. Vernon area enjoy being able to come to the museum. Admission is free. In "get-togethers" she hosts, young people flock to Adept Museum to learn from her about everything from folk dances to the space program. Vivian Ayers has also taught classes in several schools in the area.

Comparing the way she reaches and teaches young people with ways of the ancients she says, "The ancients always said, 'Myriad are the paths to success and prosperity.' And I believe that, but this is the way that we know and that our young people must go: KNOW YOUR OWN WORLDS OF BEING AND EXPRESSION; AND STAY WITHIN YOUR ELEMENT!"[7]

Interviewed for this story, the versatile writer, curator and mother made a wish that shows how unselfish she can be, and identified a person she admires as a role model. "I wish you would say something about Anna DuPree," she said. "She was a cosmetologist, a smart businesswoman who founded the Eliza Johnson home, the first home for the Black aged in Houston. She also helped organize the Houston Citizen's Chamber of Commerce, Houston's Black Chamber of Commerce, which is still going. I don't think she gets enough credit for the great work she did . . . she was an inspiration to me and many others."

Does Vivian Ayers miss living in Texas? And would she go back to Houston if her life took a turn in that direction? "In a heartbeat!" she said, smiling widely. "But that's not likely to happen, and that's O.K. because I am giving something to the community and, hopefully, helping educate and entertain. Young people who come here often leave saying that they have recovered their pride in being Black, and that gives me great satisfaction. I want to feel that the museum shares with them a vision of excellence. I also want to make a change in the hearts of people. You see, if I do, then, we'll *all* become better people."[8]

Meanwhile, when she gets homesick for Texas, she visits friends and relatives still there. But if that isn't possible, she goes to Texas without taking a trip. She steps outside into her garden, which she has designed in the shape of Texas, and within seconds she is standing wherever it is that she wants to be in the great state of Texas!

John Biggers
World-famous Artist

JOHN THOMAS BIGGERS is an outstanding artist. For about forty years he worked to build a splendid art program for students at Texas Southern University. All the while he was refusing to accept offers that would have enlarged his personal reputation.

John was born April 13, 1924, in Gastonia, Texas. His parents, Paul and Cora Biggers, had seven children. He was the youngest. When John's father, Paul, was about six years old, a tree fell on him, smashing his leg against another tree. The injured leg had to be cut off above the knee.

"We never thought of Papa as being crippled or even handicapped," John said. "He was more active and productive than any two-legged man I ever knew. He even pitched horse-shoes and played baseball with us boys."[1]

Paul Biggers was born in South Carolina in 1881. His mother, who had formerly been enslaved, was half Cherokee and half Black. His father was the white farmer who had owned Paul's mother until emancipation. However, Paul's mother was married to a man named Jim Britt, and Paul always considered him his father.

As a teenager, Paul rode a mule into North Carolina and enrolled at Lincoln Academy. This school was founded by the American Missionary Association shortly after the Civil War. Its purpose was to educate formerly enslaved people and their children. Paul and his mule stayed at Lincoln Academy until

John Biggers

13

he graduated. While he was a student at Lincoln, he met Cora Fingers, whom he married in 1909. In later years, four of the couple's children, including John, would attend Lincoln Academy.

After Cora and Paul were married, they moved to Gastonia, Texas, where Paul's twin brother, Sandy was living. Paul bought a lot across the street from Sandy and built a house on it for his family, which then included two children. As the family grew, Paul added rooms to the house.

The Biggers family had a large vegetable garden, and they had turkeys, ducks, chickens, and rabbits in their yard. Their cow was kept with the cows of their neighbors along a nearby creek. Their hogs were kept in a neighborhood hog pen about a mile away. Mama and Papa Biggers cured hams and bacon, and did the hardest work that had to be done by the family. But as soon as they could walk, the children worked in the vegetable garden, milked the cow, churned butter, and fed the hogs. Their life was filled with work, fun, reading, and studying from the many books the family owned.

However, there came a time when Gastonia passed an ordinance banning citizens from keeping chickens, cows, pigs, and other farm animals in the city. This was done to improve sanitation. But the new ordinance changed everything for the Biggers family. They had lived off the land, with little need to work for someone else. Recalling the effect of the new order on his family and the surrounding neighbors, John explained that "it broke the back of our little community. Things were never the same again."[2]

Cora Biggers started to cook, sew, wash, and iron clothes to help support the family. When her husband was ill and dying, Cora took in washing and ironing, and worked as a domestic servant. The children helped. They ran errands, did chores, hauled water from the well to fill the giant wash pots, and stoked the fires beneath the pots with wood and coal.

Just as hard as the family worked together, they played together. Among John's fondest memories are days of playing horseshoes and baseball with Papa Paul wheeling about on one leg and a crutch as fast as, or faster than, a person with two legs!

14

Papa Biggers kept a small shoe repair shop. He was a teacher at several rural schools, and he was a preacher. Throughout his life, he studied Latin and Greek. This helped him to research Bible scriptures and teach young ministers.

Paul Biggers wanted his children to love books as much as he did. Both he and his wife were determined to help their children learn all they could about the world and the people in it. So Mama and Papa Biggers made a rule that each child must read for two hours every day. They set a good example because both of them could be found reading in every spare moment.

Every night, the family read together. Papa Biggers read to the seven children, and the children read to each other. At first, John hated being made to read. Compared to his sisters and brothers, he was a slow reader. But as time went on, John came to truly enjoy reading. Before he started school, he was reading well. From books he had read at home he had made fast friends with Aesop's fables and the B'rer Rabbit tales of Joel Chandler Harris. In elementary school, John fell in love with Charles Dickens' books *A Tale of Two Cities* and *David Copperfield.*

Long, pleasant evenings at the Biggers home were filled with warmth and cheer. John constantly clung to his father. Papa Biggers had a marvelous singing voice, and he traveled through the neighborhood from house to house singing spirituals and folk songs. When he was at home, people brought their problems to him. John was always close by, happily drinking in his dad's talks with grown-ups.

For the rest of his life, John Biggers would remember what he learned of right and wrong, and good and bad, as he listened to his father talk during those warm, lovely evenings. After he became a man he would say, "It was an atmosphere of great warmth. My perception of the value of individuals came largely from my father and later was reflected in my art. This was one of the most important influences in my life."[3]

When he was only a toddler, John worked on his first art project with the help of his sisters and brothers. Every year, the Biggers children gathered clay from underneath their house and used it to build a model of the city of Gastonia. They made buildings, streets, mules, horse-drawn wagons, and cars. There were two seven-story buildings in Gastonia which the children also carefully copied. It was hard work, but what a joy it was to see the clay city of Gastonia shaped by their own hands!

Mama and Papa Biggers enrolled John at Highland Elementary School when he was four years old. He now believes the school did more for children than modern schools that fail to teach students what they must know to succeed in life. At Highland, students were drilled in reading, writing, and arithmetic until they learned those skills. And there was strict discipline. A child was not permitted to do whatever he or she wished to do without considering whether it was right or wrong, or how others would be affected.

In the second grade, John's teacher was Mrs. Blue. She became a very important teacher to him. Every day, students in Mrs. Blue's class drew pictures of birds. In those days, on every box of Arm and Hammer baking soda there was a picture of a bird. The students spent hours copying these pictures from baking soda boxes Mrs. Blue brought to class. After the children learned to copy the pictures well, they were asked to draw the birds from memory. At the end of the year, John Biggers could draw over a hundred birds from memory.

There is little doubt that John Biggers was the best artist in Mrs. Blue's class. But there were others whose art was outstanding. James Samuel Miller was one of those artists. He and John remained friends through the years. And James Miller moved on to become the principal of an elementary school in Gastonia.

While John was the only one of the Biggers children to become a professional artist, all of the Biggers children could draw. For many years, all posters at Highland Elementary School were drawn by children from the Biggers family. The eldest son, Sylvester, drew Bible scenes and pictures of Christ in beautiful color. Almost every home in the community had one of Sylvester's pictures hanging on the wall. The third son, Joe, was in Hawaii during World War II. There he made a business out of painting scenes on coconuts and selling them to tourists and men and women in military service.

If you ask John Biggers where his artistic talent came

from, he will tell you, first of all, from God. He also gives credit to his parents and his home environment. "It was the atmosphere in our home which was most important," he said, "the insistence that we respect ourselves and other people too, the insistence on high standards, the unwavering belief in right, in the truly Christian way of life. In these things I perceive the basic impulses for creativity."[4]

The atmosphere in the home was created by Mama and Papa Biggers. Mama Biggers was a warm, lovely woman who saw beauty and wonder in nature and human beings around her. She was constantly pointing out the beauty she saw to her children, and teaching them her strong moral code. She believed a person's body was God's holy temple which should not be defiled by alcohol, tobacco, tea or coffee.

Speaking of his mother, John Biggers said, "She saw beauty in practically everything and was quick to point it out to her children. The beauties and wonders of nature constantly enriched her life and ours as well. She was not an artist, but she had an artist's perception of the beautiful. The atmosphere she and Papa created in our home was an important force in my life as an artist."[5] Papa Biggers was a natural draftsman. His handwriting was beautiful, and he made excellent drawings of things he was going to build.

For many years Papa Biggers had diabetes, for which he did not receive medical treatment. After some time, his good leg became infected with gangrene and had to be amputated. After that, he lost his sight. But the love and strength that guided his spirit remained bright. Then, in 1936, the bright flame of Papa Biggers' life flickered and died.

Today John Biggers remembers his father as a great man. And he is grateful for the life his father and mother were able to provide for him and his sisters and brothers. To some extent, the Biggers family lived in their own little world. Members of the family worshiped, worked, read, studied, and played together.

Interestingly, the Biggers family and its neighbors managed to avoid much of the strife and violence between African-Americans and Caucasians that filled those years. "We never really thought much about race," John Biggers said. "The

17

Black people lived in their separate world. Ours was a close world. For the most part we took care of our own. We accepted the differences in races as a matter of fact. That's the way the world was. Usually we just stayed on our side of town.

"Nearly every Negro family had a special relationship with a white family, usually a family for whom we had worked through the years. When we encountered a problem which we couldn't handle, we usually turned to our special white friends for help, and usually got it. Anything to do with the law came in that category, for the law was controlled completely by white men. People in power have always had to speak for people out of power. I suppose it was a paternalistic relationship, a carry-over from slavery, but we didn't feel demeaned by it. The world was so different then from the way it is now that there really is no basis for comparison."[6]

After Papa Biggers died, John and Joe, his older brother, enrolled in high school courses at Lincoln Academy. To help with expenses, John worked half-time and Joe worked two-thirds of the time. Mama Biggers became a matron for girls at an African-American orphanage 200 miles from Gastonia. She used the money she earned to help educate her children through their years at college.

Lincoln Academy was six miles east of Gastonia. It consisted of three brick buildings and nine structures that were less sturdy. The school had its own farm, barns and shops, and the students had to keep everything in top condition. All pupils had to work, including those who were paying full tuition. Students repaired roads and buildings, milked cows, cared for the grounds, managed and butchered cattle, worked in the laundry.

Anyone who broke the rules was sentenced to extra work. This often meant working on rock piles, digging up rocks needed to build roads. John Biggers did more than his share to supply rocks for roads. High spirited and mischievous, he stayed in trouble. But because of his high grades he also stayed on the honor roll, so he was never sent home.

Along with his regular jobs as fireman for boiler rooms, and caretaker for the tennis courts, John worked in the carpentry shop as a cabinet maker. This was as close to art as he

18

came, and he found the work challenging and enjoyable. Indeed, his time at Lincoln was so rewarding that going to college later on was a bit of a letdown.

At Lincoln, John was active in swimming, football, basketball, baseball, and tennis. Great singers such as Marian Anderson and Roland Hayes came to the school to perform. And nationally recognized people like Walter White, head of the National Association for the Advancement of Colored People (NAACP), and the author Howard Thurman came to speak. John was happy working and learning with students, teachers, and visiting personalities. He formed a special friendship with one instructor.

"Henry Westerband became my ideal," he explained. "An athlete and musician, he could draw and paint. He put on overalls every day and worked with the students on the roads. He could work with his mind and his hands. He taught me furniture making, and heightened my sense of aesthetics in the process. The furniture we made had to be both functional and beautiful.

"The only creative work I had at Lincoln was in cabinetmaking, working from my own designs. I kept on drawing, but it was mostly copying. I didn't know what art was. Art, I thought, was making pictures. It had nothing to do with creative expression."[7]

Bill Drone was another Lincoln teacher who greatly influenced John Biggers. "He taught us living biology," Biggers said, "the interrelationship of man, plants, and animals, the meaning of the natural world.

"All my life, as I have thought of the meaning of man and of beauty — the things with which my art has been concerned — I felt that the foundations were laid in those days. Lincoln took up where Papa and Mama left off."[8]

John Biggers' appreciation of his African roots, which would revolutionize his art later on, also began at Lincoln. Black Americans were often ashamed of their heritage at that time. They believed Africans were ignorant and uncivilized without culture or history. But Dr. Henry McDowell, Lincoln's president, had lived in Angola for twenty years, and had learned that nothing could be further from the truth.

19

In John Biggers' words, "Black Americans generally thought of their African background as somehow being shameful and regarded Africans as savages. Dr. McDowell came through with a positive approach to our African heritage which was brand new to me. He brought some students from Africa to the campus. We lived intimately with them and learned to our surprise that they were basically the same as we were."[9]

After leaving Lincoln, John attended Hampton Institute in Virginia. There he met Hazel Hales, the girl he would marry. He also met Victor Lowenfeld, who would have a greater effect on John's life than any man except his father. Lowenfeld was an artist and psychologist who joined the faculty at Hampton Institute the year before John enrolled. Hampton had no art course, and Lowenfeld asked the president, Dr. Arthur Howe, to let him organize an art class. "All right, if you want to waste your time. These people aren't interested in art," Howe replied.[10]

Through a bulletin board notice, Lowenfeld announced that an art course was being offered at night. The notice said students would not receive college credits for taking the course. Just over 800 students were enrolled at Hampton Institute, and about 750 of them showed up for the art class! Lowenfeld accepted a manageable number of students, and the next year his art class was offered for credit.

Studying painting and drawing under Lowenfeld, John Biggers learned that art was more than making pictures. He discovered that art was a way of learning about himself and fulfilling his life. "I began to see art not primarily as an individual expression of talent, but as a responsibility to reflect the spirit and style of the Negro people," he said. "It became an awesome responsibility to me, not a fun thing at all."[11]

John Biggers spent some time in the navy, returned to Hampton, then moved on to Pennsylvania State University, where Lowenfeld had joined the faculty. In August 1949, John Biggers accepted an offer to organize an art department for Texas Southern University for African-Americans in Houston, Texas. He remained there until he retired in 1983. Afterward, he became a professor emeritus and continued to do important work for the school.

When John Biggers arrived at Texas Southern University, the school administration had little understanding of what an art department should be. John met great difficulties as he worked to achieve his goals for the school and its students. Nevertheless, his efforts helped many students to become outstanding artists. Even though John Biggers remained at TSU, his works of art slowly made their way around the world until he gained an exciting national reputation. His paintings and drawings won national prizes, and his illustrations appeared in many books.

In 1952, John's mother came to live with him and his wife. She remained an active, helpful part of the family until her death at the age of eighty-eight. She was buried beside her husband. At the grave site, the children of Paul and Cora Biggers remembered their father and mother and the wonderful home they had made for the family. "The family is the most important thing in the world. First, of course, your own, but equally important, the family of man," John Biggers observed.[12]

In 1956 John and Hazel Biggers visited West Africa. "It was the greatest experience of my life," John said.[13] Later, the couple made a trip to East Africa, which further expanded John's understanding of his heritage, of himself as an artist, and of the world around him. In the words of John Biggers, "My philosophy as a teacher has always been concerned with the self-identify of students. We must understand who we are and what we are. To do that we must understand our roots. We can't know where we are going unless we know where we came from, and where we are now."[14]

Mary Branch
First African-American Woman
College President in Texas

MARY BRANCH, president of Tillotson College from 1930 to 1944, was the first African-American woman to become president of a college in Texas. Records indicate it may have been nearly forty years afterward that the first white woman became president of a Texas college.

Mary was born in Farmville, Virginia, in 1881 or 1882 (historical records differ on the year). Tazewell Branch, Mary's father, was born in captivity, or slavery as it was called in America. He was a servant in the house of his captor, whom he had to call "master," as enslaved people were made to do.

Tazewell learned to read and write. As a young man, he became a skilled shoemaker. Widely respected for his intelligence and integrity, Tazewell Branch was elected to the Virginia legislature in 1874 and served for four years. However, he was greatly troubled by the corruption he observed among many politicians, and he retired from politics.

Returning to Farmville, he became a tax collector. Later, he resumed his trade as a shoemaker. But he had grown old, and it had become difficult for him to earn enough money to support his family. Harriet Branch, Mary's mother, pitched in and supported the family by doing domestic work in the community.

One of her jobs was to wash clothes for several girls and teachers at the State College in Farmville. At the age of thirteen, Mary was "attending college" in an unusual way. Later Mary would say, "I did attend the State College in Farmville, for my mother washed clothes for a number of girls and teachers, and I attended regularly to get clothes or take them!"[1]

In time, Mary completed high school at the Normal School of Virginia State College in Petersburg. She was concerned about her people. She wanted African-Americans to learn to read and speak English well.

Mary Branch

She began her teaching career as an elementary school English teacher in Blackstone, Virginia. Her salary was $27.50 a month. After awhile she was asked to join the faculty of her alma mater, Virginia State College. She consented, and was an important member of the staff for twenty years. Her position involved being housing director for male and female dormitories in addition to teaching. Her classes gained a reputation for being challenging. Tagged "Branch English" by the students, her courses were difficult, interesting, and extremely popular.

During the summers, Mary Branch attended a number of universities as an undergraduate student, including the University of Pennsylvania, Columbia University, and the University of Chicago. In 1922, she earned a bachelor of philosophy degree from the University of Chicago, and three years later a master of arts degree in English. She also began to earn credits for a doctorate in education.

After a career change that took her to a position in social studies at Sumner Junior College in Kansas City, Kansas, Mary Branch was named dean of girls at Vashon High School in St. Louis, Missouri. This was the largest school for African-American women in the nation. She had reached the top of her profession as an African-American educator, earning a substantial salary. And since Vashon was in a very poor neighborhood, she had excellent opportunities for professional and personal enrichment.

One day in 1930 her telephone rang. The American Missionary Association was calling. The association offered her a position as president of Tillotson College in Austin, Texas. She also received a similar offer from a nearby community college. It was a very difficult decision to make. Leaving her present post would mean she must give up counseling and advising young people, work which she truly enjoyed. Also, she would be giving up the largest income she had ever received. She decided to turn down both offers. The AMA called again and repeated its offer. Again she refused to accept the position.

But the American Missionary Association was persistent, and at last she agreed to take the job. She explained: "I thought of the numbers of white teachers who had gone South for years since the Civil War and worked among an alien race for no other reason than a Christian interest in the underprivileged. They had made far greater sacrifices than I would be called upon to make. I thought and prayed over the matter and finally got a definite feeling that I should go to Tillotson."[2]

Mary Branch knew that Tillotson College was a school in trouble. The institution had been established by the American Missionary Association to provide an education for African-Americans in the area of Austin, Texas. A major purpose of the organization was to develop schools throughout the South for freedmen, formerly enslaved men who had been set free after the Civil War.

Reverend George Tillotson of the AMA, a retired minister from Connecticut, toured Texas looking for a place to build another AMA school. In Austin, he found an ideal site overlooking the beautiful Colorado River. Then he raised about $16,000 and bought several acres of land upon which Tillotson Collegiate and Normal Institute was established.

The school was opened in 1881 with white administrators and teachers provided by the American Missionary Association. At first, the institution offered courses in basic studies and trades for Black students in elementary grades and high school. By 1909 the school had earned college status. It was then named Tillotson College.

However, five years later, Tillotson College began a sudden downslide. There were many reasons. Poor job opportunities, low wages, racial prejudice, racial violence, and widespread crop failure. Hoping to escape all these, Black families were leaving the South to go North. As a result, college enrollments of Black students in the South dropped, forcing some schools to make changes.

The year 1925 brought unfortunate changes to Tillotson. The institution was reduced to a junior college. Also, the American Missionary Association appointed J. T. Hodges president. Hodges was the first African-American head of Tillotson College, and he could have contributed to a brilliant chapter in its history. Instead, the new president chose to remain aloof from people in the town. This caused him to lose the support of the community.

Additional problems resulted when Hodges appointed members of his family to important college positions and they did not do their jobs well. Enrollment at Tillotson college dropped dramatically, and in 1929 President Hodges was forced to resign amidst criticisms of nepotism, dormitory irregularities, and high tuition. Because of declining enrollment and poor administration while Hodges was in charge, Tillotson converted to a women's college.

When Mary Branch arrived at Tillotson College July 1, 1930, she entered the campus through a broken down fence. The new president made her way up a scraggly path so tangled with bushes that a fox could hide in the thick undergrowth, and one was actually found hiding there. About six tired, old buildings surrounded by weather-beaten, poorly cared for mesquite trees made up the campus. Inside the administration building, Mary Branch found the president's office. It was an eight-by-ten-foot room, smaller than many utility closets.

Many people would have walked away. Not Mary Branch. She went to work like a whirlwind! First, she made a five-year plan to improve the campus and recruit new students. Then she focused on the school library, which had scarcely 2,000 appropriate books. By obtaining donations for the library, during her administration the number of books soared to more than 21,000 volumes.

Old buildings on the campus were remodeled, new edifices were erected, and the campus grounds became a showplace for lovely shrubs, trees, and athletic fields. To attract more students to the college, President Bush discontinued the high school program and developed college courses. She raised funds, doubled the staff of the faculty, and required every instructor to have a master's degree. *Pres. Branch 8/8*

Teachers were sent on tour to recruit students for Tillotson, which now provided numerous scholarships. "Play Day Activities" and sports events on campus attracted many high school girls who later became Tillotson students. Eventually, Tillotson was reorganized again as a coeducational college.

When Mary Branch arrived at Tillotson College in 1930, there were 140 students enrolled. As a result of her efforts as president, enrollments climbed. By the time of her death in 1944, more than 500 students were enrolled at the college.

The goals President Branch set for herself and the institution were achieved by working on many fronts. She involved herself and her students with neighborhood charity clubs, politics, and public schools. She worked with the faculty of the University of Texas. She also worked with the staff of Samuel Huston College, a Methodist college for African-Americans less than a mile from Tillotson College.

The two schools offered nearly the same curriculum. Both needed funds, and both needed more students. President Branch and Karl E. Downs, president of Samuel Huston College, began to share teachers, speakers, and artists. Although both Branch and Downs died before Tillotson College and Samuel Huston College merged in 1952, the two were an early force in creating the present-day Huston-Tillotson College.

In addition to her work with and for students, Mary Branch was a warrior for civil rights. She used her influence to boycott racially segregated businesses or to close Tillotson's accounts with firms that were racially segregated and businesses that showed racial prejudice.

In 1943, Mary Branch was elected president of the local chapter of the National Association for the Advancement of Colored People (NAACP). She also sponsored a student chapter of the NAACP on the campus of Tillotson College.

Approached by Dr. Frederick Patterson of Tuskegee Institute with his new idea for a United Negro College Fund, President Branch promptly enrolled Tillotson. Thus Tillotson College became one of the first colleges to join UNCF, a powerful force in obtaining money for all predominantly Black colleges.

As president of a college, Mary Branch followed a career that was extremely rare among women of her time. During the 1930s and 1940s there apparently were no Caucasian women serving as college presidents. But two African-American women followed the footsteps of Mary Branch into the office of college president: Mary McLeod Bethune and Artemisia Bowden.

Mary McLeod Bethune founded Bethune-Cookman College in Florida. Artemisia Bowden became president of Saint

Philip's College in San Antonio, Texas, after a series of promotions from her original position as an instructor. Mrs. Bethune came to world attention when President Franklin Roosevelt named her director of the Division of Negro Affairs of the National Youth Administration (NYA). She was also a member of the Committee for National Defense under President Harry Truman.

The hard work of Mary Branch as president of Tillotson College paid off. She involved herself in the lives of people and organizations near the school, and they loved and supported her and Tillotson College.

Guided by Mary Branch, the college reclimbed the ladder of national recognition. Tillotson College was awarded senior college standing by the State Board of Education in 1931, and was returned to coeducation status in 1936. Finally, in 1943 it was upgraded to an "A" rating by the Southern Association of Colleges and Secondary Schools.

As the institution advanced, the merit of its president was also being recognized. President Mary Branch received two honorary degrees from world-respected institutions of higher learning. The first, doctor of pedagogy, was bestowed on her by Virginia State College. The second, a doctor of laws degree, was awarded to Mary Branch from Howard University.

Suddenly, at the peak of her career, President Branch began to feel sick. She decided that a visit to her sisters in New Jersey might help improve her health. But during the visit she became extremely ill. She was rushed to a local hospital, where she died on July 6, 1944. As memorials to a life well lived, she left Tillotson College, the vision of Huston-Tillotson College, and the enriched lives of thousands of students who had passed her way.

Bessie Coleman
Daring Queen of the Skies

On June 19, 1925, at an air show in Houston, Texas, the crowd watched a small airplane take off, climb above the people, and zoom into a snowy cloud. The plane appeared again above the clouds and continued ascending until it seemed to be the size of a toy. Suddenly it swooped around and plunged toward the ground, hurtling to within a few feet of the earth before the pilot broke the dizzying fall, pulled the aircraft up, and streaked away!

A roar of relief, admiration and pride rolled through the largely African-American crowd. BESSIE COLEMAN, America's only Black aviatrix, was flying that plane. High in the air she dived again, barrel rolled the aircraft, did figure eights and loop the loops. This was a wonderful Juneteenth celebration!

On this date in 1865, a United States government ship had sailed into the port of Galveston, Texas, with Gen. Gordon Granger. The general came ashore and read the Emancipation Proclamation, which President Lincoln had signed two and a half years earlier. The proclamation said slavery had ended and people who had been enslaved were free. Thus, Africans held captive in Texas became the last enslaved people in the country to be told they were free. Afterwards, Black Texans commemorated the date as "Juneteenth," the first African-American holiday.

The years after the first Juneteenth were filled with racial violence, discrimination, and Jim Crow laws. African-Americans were told they were inferior to other races. They were often not permitted to vote, or buy land or property. There were laws against Aframericans attending the same schools, or using the same train coaches, restrooms, restaurants, hotels, or water fountains used by whites. African-Americans who protested risked being tarred and feathered, whipped, or lynched.

Now, here was Bessie Coleman, "Queen Bess" they called her, high above the clouds for all the world to see, giving the lie to the belief that African-Americans were not equal to other people. A small, beautiful Black woman of thirty-three, with her looping, swooping, diving airplane, she was lighting up the skies, exclaiming, "Look at me!" Proclaiming, "We can do anything! *Anything!! ANYTHING!!!*"

She was born in 1892, in Atlanta, Texas, the daughter of Susan and George Coleman, who had many other children. When Bessie was two, the family moved to Waxahachie, Texas, and at six, she started school. Bessie walked four miles to school, where one teacher taught students from first to eighth grade.

Sometimes it was not easy to study. There were too many children in a class, and too few books, papers, and pencils. Also, the building was cold in winter and hot in summer. But Bessie liked to learn, and soon she was an outstanding student in math.

When she was nine years old, her father moved to Oklahoma without his family, and life changed for Bessie. George Coleman wanted to get away from racial prejudice in Texas. He believed he and his family would be better off in Oklahoma, and he asked his wife to move there with him. However, she refused. After he left, his wife became housekeeper and cook for a white family. While Susan Coleman was at work, Bessie took care of the home and the younger children.

Often Bessie could not go to school because she was doing chores or picking cotton. During cotton-picking season, schools for Black children closed so they could join their families and pick cotton in the fields. Since the cotton picking season varied depending on the weather, in some years Black children did not attend school from late July until December. As a result, Bessie missed a great deal of important class work. Although she grew to be an extremely intelligent woman, her weak elementary school background sometimes showed in the spelling and grammar of letters she wrote.

Bessie was not much help when her family picked cotton. Pickers put cotton in long bags that dragged along the ground, and one time Bessie was caught riding on the sack of

Bessie Coleman

the person picking cotton in front of her! Whenever an airplane was heard approaching in the distance, her relatives started to laugh, knowing Bessie would stop working to watch the plane fly over the field.

Dreams of being an airplane pilot were shaping her life and touching people around her. As time went on, parents of some white playmates discovered their children were securing information about aviation for Bessie. One child's father tested Bessie on aerodynamics. To his surprise, her scientific knowledge of the skies was above average.

This man and the pastor of Bessie's church, Missionary Baptist Church, wanted to help her become a flyer. They tried to arrange for Bessie to begin her studies at a nearby airfield. However, the pilots laughed and scorned the idea. They said a Black woman could never become an airplane pilot.

Bessie spent much of her time reading books her mother rented from the traveling "wagon library." Many stories were about Black men and women who achieved greatness. Sometimes she would wake one of her sisters at three in the morning to talk about what she had read, and what she wanted to do with her life.

She was now certain she would have to leave Waxahachie to become a flyer. If only she could join her brother, Walter, who lived in Chicago, Bessie was sure she could find a flying school or a teacher. But she didn't even have train fare. Members of Bessie's church decided to help. They raised money and sent her to Chicago.

Bessie's rise to the skies did not happen overnight. Six years passed after she arrived in Chicago before she became a flyer. Meanwhile, to earn a living, she became a manicurist, and later managed a chili house. She also married a man named Claude Glenn so quietly that many of her relatives never knew about him.

The search for a flying instructor in Chicago was not successful. One after the other, the flyers Bessie approached turned her down. Finally, in desperation she went to Robert Abbott, publisher and editor of the *Chicago Defender,* an African-American newspaper.

Since there were no African-American flyers in Chicago,

Abbott knew the airmen that had rebuffed Bessie had done so because of her race and because she was a woman. Abbott advised Bessie to go to France, where he said she would not be discriminated against.

With the newspaperman's help, Bessie traveled to France and earned her aviator's license from the Federation Aeronautique Internationale, one of the finest aviation schools in the world. She received her pilot's license in 1921, two years before the famous aviatrix Amelia Earhart received hers.

For the rest of her short life, "Queen Bess" never stopped moving toward higher goals. She took more flying lessons, organized air shows, worked to open an aviation school, and toured America speaking about flying.

Other Aframericans were inspired to follow in her footsteps and make their dreams come true. Among them was Bessie's nephew, Arthur Freeman, who became an aviator. When he was eight years old, he attended an air show and watched Bessie's amazing stunt flying. Nobody in the huge crowd had reason to notice the small, wide-eyed boy until he shouted in a voice bursting with pride, *"That's my aunt!"*

In February 1923, Bessie purchased an airplane which stalled and crashed during a twenty-five-mile flight she was making. She was seriously injured, but she sent a message to her fans from her hospital bed: "Tell them all that as soon as I can walk, I'm going to fly!" It was many months before the pioneering aviator walked again, but true to her word, she also began to fly again.

In April 1926, Bessie's career and her life ended in Jacksonville, Florida, as the second airplane she purchased was being tested for an air show. She had asked aviator William Wills to fly her plane from the front cockpit as she peered over the edge of the back cockpit. She was searching the field below, looking for a jump site on which to land in an air show the next day. Her seat belt was not fastened because she was too small to look over the side with the belt holding her down.

The plane was cruising at eighty miles an hour when it suddenly speeded up to 110 miles an hour, nose dived, went into a tailspin, and flipped upside down. Bessie fell to her death. With his seat belt fastened, Wills struggled to control the plane. However, he failed to regain control. The aircraft plunged to the ground and he too was killed.

Controversy surrounds Bessie Coleman's death. Millions loved her, but she had made enemies. At a time when laws kept Caucasian and Black races from being together, Bessie refused to hold racially segregated air shows. She also would not fly in racially segregated shows given by others. This angered many people.

The plane crash was caused by a loose wrench which slid into the controls of the aircraft and jammed the mechanism. Some say the wrench was left "adrift" purposely; others believe it was left loose by accident.

There are people who think Bessie's plane was sabotaged by spiteful Caucasian fliers who hated being outclassed by an Aframerican woman. Others point the finger at William Wills. They picture him as a jealous colleague or rejected lover who intended to cause Bessie's death and then save himself.

When Robert Abbott heard that Wills was going to fly with Bessie, he was alarmed. The *Chicago Defender* publisher did not trust the Texas flyer. Something in the pilot's face seemed to warn Abbott of trouble. He told Bessie how he felt and asked her not to fly with Wills. He said she should get another partner for her flight. But Bessie disregarded his advice.

Wills had flown the plane from Texas to Florida. Flimsy and poorly built, like many planes of that time, it had malfunctioned and stalled twice, causing Wills to make two forced landings. Nevertheless, in spite of the aircraft's poor record, many believed Wills had purposely speeded up the plane while Bessie wasn't wearing her seat belt. They insist he planned for Bessie to be ejected, believing he could land the plane safely afterward.

Until this day, Bessie Coleman's death is clouded in mystery. However, the life of daring "Queen Bess" remains a brilliant meteor which will shine in the skies of history forever.

Wilhelmina Ruth Fitzgerald Delco

State Legislator and
"Patron Saint of Education"

Her name is WILHELMINA RUTH FITZGERALD DELCO, and she has devoted much of her life to increasing educational opportunities for people in Texas. To the people of Texas, she is the "Patron Saint of Education." To her eight grandchildren she is "Granna." And their Granna is a really fun person with enough love to wrap around all of them.

She has almost one hundred pretty lapel pins shaped like different kinds of bumblebees that the grandchildren like to see and touch. Some are quite inexpensive, but many of the bee pins are decorated with jewels. They have beautiful diamonds, pearls or other precious stones for eyes, or they have jewels sprinkled on their heads or wings. One has wings that move.

Granna likes bees a lot because they are always busy. People know she likes them, so they give her bee pins. But most of the pins are gifts from the children's grandfather. They call him "Grandel." On special days like birthdays and Christmas, Grandel gives Granna a bee pin. Even though they are only pins, the bees remind her to keep busy serving the community. The bee pins also remind the grandchildren that serving the community will be a good thing for them to do as soon as they are able.

On July 16, 1929, Wilhelmina Ruth Fitzgerald was born in Chicago, Illinois. Her father was a court bailiff, and her mother was a probation officer. There were five children in the Fitzgerald family, and Wilhelmina was the eldest.

By the time she was twelve years old, her parents were divorced. Nevertheless, her mother constantly talked with her children about the value of obtaining a solid education. Supported by their mother, and their determination to study and achieve, all of the children in the Fitzgerald family attended college and received various professional degrees.

35

When Wilhelmina was a high school senior, William Dawson, Chicago's nationally known congressman, took an interest in her college plans. He arranged for Wilhelmina to receive a full scholarship to the University of Illinois at Champaign. This largely white university had dormitories in which only white students lived. Congressman Dawson wanted Wilhelmina to be the first African-American student to live in a dormitory of the University of Illinois. However, that did not happen.

Wilhelmina attended Wendell Phillips High School in Chicago. She was president of the student body and a member of the National Honor Society. As a senior at Wendell Phillips, she debated a student from another school during a mass meeting of Chicago high school pupils. Angry because Wilhelmina and her associates disagreed with his point of view, the student accused them of being communists. This label was used by many people during that time to frighten and quiet anyone who disagreed with what they said.

However, Wilhelmina Ruth Fitzgerald refused to sit still and swallow the put-down as many people would have. Instead, she told the student if he could not handle a disagreement without calling names, he had no business being at the meeting!

The dispute was reported in Chicago's newspapers, and Congressman Dawson read about his protege's forceful remarks. The congressman decided that enrollment at the University of Illinois was not the best plan for such a strong spirited student.

The phone rang, and Congressman Dawson was on the line. The newspaper story was on his mind, and young Miss Fitzgerald was in for a surprise.

"Oh, no," he said, speaking of his original plan for a scholarship at the University of Illinois. "No, no, no-ooooo. Let us rethink this. I don't want to have to be getting you out of jail every week! I'm going to recommend you to my alma mater. I went to Fisk University in Tennessee. That will be a much better situation for you."

Congressman Dawson's new plan turned out to be a tremendous blessing. Wilhelmina flourished at Fisk University, a school operated and attended primarily by African-Ameri-

Wilhelmina Ruth Fitzgerald Delco

cans. She took major courses in sociology, and minor studies in economics and business administration.

At Fisk University she met and fell in love with Exalton Delco, a tall, handsome Texan. The two married and moved to Houston, where he accepted a teaching position at Texas Southern University. Later, he enrolled as a graduate student of zoology at the University of Texas, and the couple moved to Austin to be near the university.

However, in those days, married Black students were not accepted in University of Texas housing. University officials suggested that Exalton Delco move into an Austin housing project. But he wanted better surroundings for his family, which then included three children, and he arranged to live in quarters at Huston-Tillotson College. After completing his courses at the University of Texas, he joined the faculty of Huston-Tillotson College.

During the years that the Delcos were working to uplift educational standards, they were also rearing four children, Deborah, Exalton III, Loretta, and Cheryl. The husband and wife had a plan for naming their children. They wanted the first letters of the children's names to spell "DELCO." After Cheryl was born, only the letter "O" was missing.

"Sometimes people ask me 'Where is little Octavia?'" the proud mother laughs. "I always tell them that 'O' is not for 'Octavia.' 'O' stands for 'it's *Over!*'"

Wilhelmina Delco became active in education when her children were in elementary school. That was her way of making sure Austin's public schools provided her children with the best education possible. For six years, beginning in 1968, she was a School Board trustee. Then she was elected to the Texas House of Representatives.

In both places, Wilhelmina was always at the front of every battle to improve education. As a result, she earned key positions with educational programs in Texas and across the country. Because of her dedication and hard work, people in Texas and the nation came to think of Wilhelmina Delco as the "Patron Saint of Education." Her commitment earned her an appointment as chairwoman of the Higher Education Committee of the Texas legislature.

She was head of the Higher Education Committee from 1979 until 1991. Then she was appointed Speaker Pro Tempore of the House of Representatives. The Speaker of the House is leader of the Texas House of Representatives. The Speaker Pro Tempore is second in command and presides when the Speaker of the House is unable to be present. Representative Delco was the first and only woman ever appointed to that post.

During her years in the Texas House of Representatives, she initiated more than a hundred bills. Most of these bills were related to education. Some are legislative landmarks. One extremely important piece of legislation she helped bring about is known as "No pass, no play." It prevented students who performed poorly in their classroom studies from playing in extracurricular school sports. This let everyone know that in obtaining an education, class work is more important than athletic games.

Legislation co-sponsored by Representative Delco reduced class size to twenty-two students. Before that, thirty or more students were allowed in a class. When the popular representative retired, in 1995, Richard Kouri, president of the Texas State Teachers Association, praised her highly.

Kouri said it was impossible to know how much money Texas schools had received as a result of the efforts of Representative Delco. He stated that "in the past four years public education funding has increased about seven billion dollars, probably a larger increase for the same period than any time in Texas history!"[1]

Representative Delco sponsored a change in the Texas Constitution which permitted Prairie View A&M University, a small largely African-American school, to receive more money from the Permanent University Fund. This fund of over a billion dollars had been kept mostly for the use of the University of Texas at Austin and Texas A&M at College Station.

"This was my greatest achievement!" the beautiful mother of four exclaimed triumphantly. She is also proud of her reputation for intelligence, integrity, and honesty, and her record of standing for truth and right against all opposition. "I haven't done anything that the people of my district are ashamed of," she once said.

Much more than that, what she had done made people respect and love her, made them proud and happy. These people included voters who elected her to represent them time and again, officials of the city, state and nation, her friends and her family.

To show how much she was loved and appreciated, many of these people got together and gave a huge celebration in her honor when she retired. Hundreds attended, among them government officials, heads of organizations, family members, friends, and just plain folks. Telegrams were read from the highest office holders in the country, including President Bill Clinton.

Students from schools she had helped performed in her honor. Elementary schools, high schools, colleges and universities were on the program, as were members of her family. Speeches, poems, music, and creative dances paid special tribute to Wilhelmina Ruth Fitzgerald Delco who had worked her way into the hearts of her city, state, and nation.

Dr. Charles Hines of Prairie View A&M University announced that a new classroom building would be named for Wilhelmina Ruth Fitzgerald Delco. Representatives of Austin Community College, Huston-Tillotson College, and the University of Texas announced that scholarships were being established at their schools in the name of Wilhelmina Delco or in the names of Wilhelmina Delco and her husband, Dr. Exalton Delco.

Dr. Delco, who earned his doctorate in zoology, had also made a worthy contribution to education. Through the years he was part of the faculty or administration of several educational institutions, including Austin Community College, Huston-Tillotson College, Texas Southern University, and the University of Texas.

Upon retiring, State Representative Delco did not stop working. In her private life, she and her husband of forty-two years shared in caring for her mother and his mother in their home. Publicly, the former representative became a legislator emeritus, and remained a nationally respected leader in education.

In addition, she continued to serve on a number of committees and boards of directors. For instance, she continued to be active in creating Vision Village. This project, which she conceived, was designed to build a community of people of different ages acting with and for each other. Her idea was to use a large, landscaped area to build a school, and living quarters for elderly people, young mothers, and small children. As people from the different groups went about daily life, they would naturally help and learn from one another.

Added to all this, Ms. Delco expects that in her retirement years she will have more time to sew for her grandchildren. Ever since they were born, sewing for them has been an important part of her life and theirs. Every year at Christmas and Easter, each of her grandchildren is given a special holiday outfit made by Granna. On the evening of their Granna's retirement celebration, all of her grandchildren went on stage and shared in reciting a tribute to their grandmother. Wearing gorgeous shirts, ties, vests, coats, dresses, jackets, skirts, and blouses all made by Granna, one by one, Kwasi, Selena, Selom, Camille, Jimmy, Amina, Iris, and Simone went to the microphone and spoke. The children ranged in age from twenty-three months to twelve years. Some were too tiny to reach the microphone even when it was lowered. Others would soon be young adults.

They recited a poem composed by the former state representative's daughter, Cheryl Delco Sawyer, communications manager for ARC of Texas (an organization which helps people who are mentally retarded). The poem was written from information provided by the children:

ALL: Good evening to all of you. Our Granna is an outstanding leader with energy. But to us, she's our Granna. And here is what she means to us:

KWASI (age 12): My name is Kwasi Agbottah and "G" is for Granna's Great cooking.

SELENA (age 12): My name is Selena Edelen and "R" is for the way Granna makes birthday celebrations Really fun.

SELOM (age 12): My name is Selom Agbottah and "A" is for the way Granna makes her house A great place to spend the night.

41

CAMILLE (age 9): My name is Camille Edelen and "N" is for the Neat personalized outfits Granna sews for us during the holidays, Christmas and Easter. We are wearing them now.

AMINA (age 4): My name is Amina Sawyer and "N" is for the Neat green gum that Granna gives me for being a sweet girl.

JAMES (age 4): My name is Jimmy Sawyer and "A" is for the way that Granna is A great bedtime storyteller.

IRIS (age 4): My name is Iris Edelen and I added another "A" because Granna has All kinds of fun earrings to play with.

ALL: WE LOVE YOU GRANNA!

After the last line of the poem, Simone Sawyer, less than two years old, was told to blow a kiss or say bye bye to the audience. Simone toddled to the microphone and gurgled something. Probably no one in the audience understood her words, but everyone understood what she meant. Everyone present also felt the love these grandchildren were expressing for their precious Granna.

Speaking from her heart, the Honorable Wilhelmina Ruth Fitzgerald Delco reacted to the tributes from her grandchildren and others on the program. She warmly thanked everyone for the love and support they had given her during twenty-six years.

She ended her remarks by responding to a song performed by the Charles Gilpin Players of Prairie View A&M University. "You are the Wind Beneath My Wings," the group sang, with each singer looking and extending a hand toward her.

"My strength came from all of you," the retiring state representative told the audience, her voice alive with feeling. "You have always been the wind beneath my wings."

Then, speaking of the future, she added, "Sometimes I will be the wind beneath your wings helping you to soar. But sometimes I will be a voice whispering in your ear, still involved in what I think is the finest community in the world!"

Three Divas on Stage

What an exciting moment! Seventy-five special women were being honored for their achievements. The honorees had been recognized in *Black Texas Women,* a book by Ruthe Winegarten.[1] The stage of the auditorium of the LBJ[2] Library in Austin, Texas, was crowded with choirs and choral groups from churches, schools, and community organizations. There were choirs from Huston-Tillotson College and the University of Texas, five community choruses, singers from the alumnae of Smith College, and singers from over thirty churches.

This was a dream being brought to life by Betty Crutcher and Jennifer Whitmore, volunteers for the University of Texas. They had invited singers from far and wide to participate in a joyous musical salute to the women in the book. What happened was as wonderful as their dream.

A host of singers beautifully robed in black were powerfully directed by Reverend Irma Jones. Reverend Jones had written the words for "A Salute to Texas Women," a stirring tribute that was sung. Distinguished musicians accompanied the singers. Margaret Perry and Geneva Rawlins[3] were the pianists. Gloria Quinn was the organist.

"Magnify the Lord," an anthem composed by Virgie Carrington DeWitty, crowned the concert. A young soprano soloist began the piece a cappella. Dr. Beulah Agnes Curry Jones followed, singing in the alto range of her superb dramatic soprano voice. The angelic blend of the two voices combined with the voices of the choir singers in an explosion of song. The selection closed as it began with the soprano soloist singing alone. For a split second she paused before ending the song. Then the final note left her throat and soared. High, full, clear, beautiful. The sound rang out until it filled the room, and echoed up until it reached the rafters, sending chills through the bodies of listeners.

After the melodious tone died away, the audience sat in stunned silence for a long moment. Then thunderous applause broke out! The applause was for the wonderful gift of music the listeners had been given by the choirs, and by the

43

three divas who were on stage. The audience was praising the powerful music and spiritual presence of Dr. Virgie Carrington DeWitty, the "Diva Triumphant" (see story which follows), the magnificent aura and talent of Dr. Beulah Agnes Curry Jones, the "Grand Diva" (see story which follows), and the marvelous vitality and contribution of the youthful soprano soloist, one of several "Rising Divas."

Dr. Virgie Carrington DeWitty
The Diva Triumphant

DR. VIRGIE CARRINGTON DeWITTY will live forever as a "Diva Triumphant." Though she passed from this life in 1980, she is still living through her music that continues to thrill the world. She also lives through musicians she taught and inspired, and through an estate fund she created to aid African-American musicians.

Her plan to aid musical artists was outlined in handwritten papers read after her death. In these papers, she requested Austin's Black Arts Alliance to use a $59,000 fund from her estate to provide scholarships and loans for Aframerican music students and professional musicians.

"Magnify the Lord," and "Look Where the Lord has Brought Us" are examples of eternal music written by Virgie Carrington DeWitty. These joyous songs of praise are played and sung in the United States and in faraway nations.

She was born in Wetumka, Oklahoma, into the highly respected Carrington family. When Virgie was small, the family moved to Austin, Texas, and joined Ebenezer Baptist Church. Her mother, Violet Mercer Carrington, sang with the church choir for forty-eight years. She also played three instruments for the church orchestra: the trombone, the violin, and the coronet.

Influenced by her musical home, Virgie began to play the

44

Dr. Virgie Carrington DeWitty

piano by ear soon after she began to walk. When she was six years old, the Sunday school of Ebenezer Church had no pianist. One cold Sunday morning Violet Carrington led her young daughter to the Sunday school piano. Virgie climbed upon the piano seat, and her little-girl legs dangled above the floor as she played her first piano solo, "Jesus Wants Me for a Sunbeam."

After that, Virgie played the same song over and over every Sunday until at last the Sunday school superintendent promised to give her a birthstone ring if she would learn another tune!

It was a perfect beginning for her career. For the rest of her life, Virgie Carrington DeWitty was indeed a sunbeam shining rays of musical light, as she played the piano, sang, and taught in churches, schools, and conventions in Austin and distant places.

After attending Austin public schools, she furthered her education at Phillips White Private Academy, Huston-Tillotson College, and Prairie View A&M College. Additional studies were pursued at the American Conservatory of Music in Chicago, Boulder University in Boulder, Colorado, Juilliard School of Music in New York, and the University of Texas at Austin.

"Little Miss," as she was called by close friends, was minister of music at Ebenezer Baptist Church for almost fifty years. During that time she wrote well over seventy anthems, gospel songs, and hymns. Many of these songs were sung by the Bright and Early Choir, which she directed every Sunday morning from Ebenezer throughout the 1930s. This group sang on the first Aframerican commercially sponsored radio program in Texas.

In addition to her church ministry, she taught private lessons in voice and piano for many years. She also taught music at Anderson High School in Austin, where she wrote the lyrics and music for the school song, "Dear Old A.H.S. We Love You." And she directed mass choirs for state, national, and international gatherings. Once, she directed a 1,500 voice chorus at the Houston Astrodome for the National Baptist Convention of America (NBCA). She was music director for NBCA for over twenty years.

Many of today's outstanding musicians were students of Virgie Carrington DeWitty. They learned much from her, and she inspired them to make outstanding contributions to music. Dr. Beulah Agnes Curry Jones was informally taught and groomed by Dr. DeWitty. This great dramatic soprano soloist, who has followed in the path of Diva Triumphant DeWitty, delights in sharing memories of her mentor.

"Little Miss was *ageless,*" she said, recalling the days when she was a young girl being informally coached by the famous Grand Diva, and singing in choirs under her supervision. "When she said, 'My dears, this is how we will sing this,' everyone did, and it was always an uplift and inspiration."

Grand Diva DeWitty has passed from this life to become a Diva Triumphant. She is no longer physically alive on the stage when choirs are singing her music. Her spiritual presence, however, seems to strongly pervade the atmosphere, uplifting and inspiring those singing and those hearing her wonderful songs.

Dr. Beulah Agnes Curry Jones
The Grand Diva

DR. BEULAH AGNES CURRY JONES is often considered the first lady of music of Austin, Texas. This artist of many talents thrills and inspires audiences as a soloist, pianist, and organist. Whenever a concert curtain rises in the capital city, there is a great possibility that the dramatic soprano voice of this "Grand Diva" will uplift an audience through a performance on stage. At other times, her knowledge and skills are at work behind concert scenes. But there are also many times when her expertise is central to what is happening both behind the scenes *and* on the stage of a concert.

A lifelong resident of Austin, Beulah Agnes Curry Jones is director of the department of music at Huston-Tillotson

College. She also functions on special music committees for Ebenezer Baptist Church. "I was born in Ebenezer," she smiled. "My parents were already members before I was born, and my church membership has been with Ebenezer since I was approximately seven or eight years of age."

The professional career of this extraordinary musical artist was also born at Ebenezer. At the age of five, she began to take piano lessons from Mrs. J. C. Lott, wife of the pastor of Ebenezer Baptist Church. In addition, the young student's mother, Mrs. Beulah M. Thompson, was a member of the Bright and Early Choir directed by Dr. Virgie Carrington DeWitty, then a Grand Diva. Young Beulah Agnes came to know and admire Grand Diva DeWitty through her mother's association with the choir. It soon became her dream to "sit at the feet" of DeWitty and then follow in her footsteps.

It wasn't long before her dream began to come true. The five-year-old diligently studied everything she was taught by Mrs. Lott. By the time she was ten, she was also a member of the Youth Choir of the church, striving to master whatever she saw Minister of Music DeWitty do and everything she heard her teach. The little girl's dedication and thirst for knowledge soon attracted the special interest of the Grand Diva.

By this time, Grand Diva DeWitty was Austin's first lady of song. Music she had composed had begun to travel around the world. "I am honored and humbled to say that I was one of her protégés," Dr. Jones recalled. "I was not a formal student of hers, but she constantly taught me, and coached me informally in singing and playing the piano."

One day, Mrs. DeWitty gave this special student a special gift. It was a curler bonnet. When Beulah Agnes showed it to her mother she said, "Treasure it, Aggie. Treasure it."

Not only was the gift treasured through the years, but every bit of knowledge she had gained from the great Grand Diva was treasured and hoarded until it could be shared with others. "I have been benefitted by everything she taught me," she said.

Years as Mrs. DeWitty's protégé were followed by years of studying music at Prairie View A&M College, Huston-Tillotson College, Texas Southern University, the University

48

Dr. Beulah Agnes Curry Jones

of Texas, and the University of Houston. She also traveled and studied in many European countries.

As the years went on, to many music lovers Dr. Beulah Agnes Curry Jones seemed to become the heir apparent to Dr. Virgie Carrington DeWitty's role as Austin's most accomplished soloist, musician, and educator. Now, in the eyes of many people, Dr. Jones is Austin's first lady of song — Austin's "Grand Diva."

Her awards include being named "Marcet Hines King Music Professor" of Huston-Tillotson College in 1986, and "Entertainer of the Year" by the Texas Legislative Black Caucus in 1989. Two years later, President Joseph T. McMillan of Huston-Tillotson College selected her to receive the "President's Faculty Achievement Award."

At this time in her career, she has the joy of having many of her former students return to say, "Thank you for doing so much to make my life successful." Recently, one young man traveled more than a hundred miles just to say thank you. Another, on his way to perform as a soloist in Morocco, stopped in Austin to see her and thank her for making his success possible.

In addition to hearing from former students, family members of previous scholars seek her out. They also tell her how much they appreciate her work. She is delighted and honored when that happens.

Asked to explain her philosophy of life, she thought for a long time, then said, *"Continue to learn, and continue to share."* It is a way of living that she practices well. And all who surround her are continually blessed as she lives out her philosophy in her daily life.

Rising Divas

(Left)
HELANIA VASHTI JOHNSON, mezzo soprano. Like many rising divas, Helania's goal is to become a performing soloist. She studied vocal musical performance at Huston-Tillotson College in Austin for four years. During her senior college year, she took minor courses in business at Oral Roberts University in Tulsa, Oklahoma. She plans to graduate from Huston-Tillotson with the Class of 1996.

(Right)
MELANIE DELIA RUTH WILKINSON, soprano. A graduate student of vocal musical performance at Southwest Texas State University with minor studies in education. Explaining that her objective is to teach music, she says, "I want to take all of my training and concert experience into the classroom."

51

Matthew (Matt) Gaines
Reconstruction Era Politician

This is the story of MATTHEW (MATT) GAINES. He was an African-American born in captivity, or slavery as it was called in America. Gaines was a senator in the state of Texas shortly after the Civil War, which ended slavery in the United States.

During the first years following the war, the country went through a time of change, or "reconstruction." Caucasian and Black people were learning to live together in new ways. White members of the Master Class could no longer hold Africans in bondage to work for them. And Africans who had been enslaved were making new lives as free men and women. Few of them owned money, property, or tools with which to work, so it was extremely hard to make successful changes.

Nevertheless, they learned to do many things well that they had not been permitted to do while in captivity. In the South, many former captives were elected to political offices. These men made outstanding contributions that remain a part of the foundation of present-day United States government.

Matt Gaines was elected to the Texas Senate in 1870. But in 1874, he was ousted from his senate seat in a way that probably would not happen as easily today. Many people believe that if Matt had had money to hire lawyers to fight for him, he could have kept his seat in the senate.

While he was a senator, Matt Gaines was informed, energetic, purposeful, and wise. Stories often picture Black politicians of the Reconstruction period with characteristics exactly the opposite of these. Gaines guarded the interests of African-Americans and worked to improve conditions for everyone regardless of race.

Gaines' election to the Texas Senate was tied to Radical Republicans who had helped mobilize Black voters. Even so, he refused to allow the political organization to tell him what to do. Because he was a Black senator and could not be controlled by his political party, Matt Gaines had enemies in high places. Politicians, newspaper editors, and influential citizens worked to destroy his influence and rob him of his senate seat.

To Gaines' surprise and disappointment, his enemies included people who had taken brave risks to help end slavery and afterward to improve the lives of people formerly enslaved. Ferdinand Flake was an example. He was a Galveston newspaper editor who had fought for the right of formerly enslaved people to vote. In 1871, however, Flake wrote an editorial to say he disapproved of attempts by the African-American man to "offensively intrude himself into the white man's house, the white man's carriage, the white man's social enjoyment, and the white man's offices."[1]

Matthew Gaines was born to an enslaved mother on a small estate plantation in Pineville, Louisiana, in 1840. He and his mother were owned by Madam Despallier, a Spanish-speaking woman with a French-Creole husband. In the Despallier house, English, French, and Spanish were spoken. According to Gaines' descendants, as an adult he spoke seven languages.

Later in life, Gaines told his son he had learned to read by the light of a candle crouched down among corn stalks. He said the books he used were sneaked to him by a white boy who also lived on the estate. Gaines never explained who the boy was. It is possible that the boy was Madam Despallier's grandson, who may also have been Gaines' half brother.

Gaines' paternity was not known. His father could have been an enslaved man who had been sold away from the mother and son. Or he may have been a captive from another plantation. And it is possible that Madam Despallier's son, the father of her grandson, was also the father of Matt Gaines.[2]

After Madam Despallier died, Matt and his mother were sold as part of her estate. They were bought by a trader who took them to the New Orleans slave market. There Matt was put up for auction and purchased by a man from Louisiana. Matt escaped. He was captured again and returned to his owner, who sold him to someone else.

This time he was bought by a Texas cotton planter. Again

Matthew (Matt) Gaines

Matt escaped, and he headed for Mexico. He was recaptured by a company of Rangers. The Rangers held him in the area of Fredericksburg, Texas, until the end of the Civil War.[3]

In 1871, Gaines made a speech that explained why he could never be a Democrat, and told how he felt about being enslaved: "When I study the laws of 1856 and 7 [1857], I can't be a Democrat. I can remember when old Master gave me 500 lashes and said he only raised the ashes on me, and next time he would reach the clean dirt. And when they could brand me with the letter C, and the Democrats made these laws, and would not open the school house door to us and we had to ask leave to marry and get a pass to go half a mile, and if it was not spelt out all grammerly [sic] the patrollers would whip you for that."[4]

Other statements Gaines made about his life in captivity indicated he worked in the fields, and that he had been a preacher. Sometimes he told his wife and children how he used to disguise himself as a woman to get off the Despallier estate to preach. He said he would put on a dress and sunbonnet and drive a buckboard to another plantation. A small, slender man, about five feet tall, the patrollers never stopped him or saw through his disguise.

In 1867, Gaines married Fanny Sutton. Afterward, a visiting bishop told the couple their marriage was invalid because the minister who performed the ceremony had not been ordained at the time. The bishop said Gaines and Fanny Sutton must repeat the ceremony with an ordained minister if they wanted to be legally married. However, by 1869, the couple had separated and no longer wished to remarry each other.

Gaines married Elizabeth Harrison in 1870, considering this as his first marriage. Of course, he did not divorce Fanny Sutton because he believed that he had never legally married her. This innocent mistake would result in a bigamy trial which would cost him his senate seat.

In 1870, the number of African-Americans in the Texas legislature included eleven representatives and two senators, Matthew Gaines and George T. Ruby. Both were hard-working, effective senators, but they were very different from each other.

Ruby had migrated from the urban North. Born in New

York City in 1841, he had grown up in Maine and been educated there. After coming to the South in 1864, he worked as a travel agent. He was also the principal of schools operated by the Freedman's Bureau in Louisiana.

George Ruby moved to Galveston, Texas, in 1866. Shortly afterward, he was elected to the 1868-69 Constitutional Convention by voters from the Galveston district, most of whom were white. He was elected to the Texas Senate in 1869. There his diplomatic skill and educated manner earned the respect of his political friends and opponents alike.

Previously enslaved and self-educated, Gaines was not like any of the other African-American members of the legislature. Most of them served quietly and subserviently. Gaines, however, made it clear from his first year in office that he considered himself the spokesman for African-American people in Texas. His efforts on their behalf attracted a loyal following among his Black constituents and made powerful enemies for him in the senate.

Throughout the Reconstruction era in Texas, African-American voters were threatened, injured, and often killed. Harassment to influence Black voters, or prevent them from voting, was an ongoing problem during the 1869 election, and it continued through the election of 1873.

The federal government provided no assistance, and the Texas legislature was divided about the necessity of preventing unfair voting practices. Concerned for the safety of Black voters and freedmen, and the rising crime rate, Gaines supported two controversial bills recommended by the governor. The bills called for the organization of two racially integrated forces to handle "extreme emergencies" and individual law breakers.

Gaines' passionate speech in favor of passing these bills was criticized by B. J. Pridgen, a moderate Republican. Pridgen mocked Gaines for his "theatrical mode" and "earnest gesticulations," and suggested that he was ignorant.

Like many Black American legislators of his time, Gaines worked to promote the welfare of all citizens. For example, during his first year as a senator, he fought strongly for frontier defense although not many African-Americans were living on the southern and western frontiers of Texas. In a de-

56

bate on the frontier defense bill, he said: "I am astonished to think that this Legislature has been here for such a period of time without passing any laws that will protect the people on the frontiers. . . . I feel the interest of people of Texas. Let me tell the Republicans that they will have to wake up out of their drowsy sleep . . . and speedily legislate for the benefit of the people at large in this state."[5]

Gaines attracted wide attention for advocating the immigration of Africans and Black Americans to Texas. Most Texans wanted people to immigrate to Texas, but they had white immigrants in mind. A bill was proposed which provided for agents in the north of the United States, western Europe, and Britain to encourage immigration to Texas.

Pointing out that no agents were to be stationed in places where dark-skinned people lived, Gaines offered an amendment which would provide for an agent to encourage immigration from Africa to Texas. His amendment was voted down.

Concerned about the lack of equality for all people in public transportation facilities, he introduced an equal accommodations bill which also failed to pass. He introduced another bill designed to encourage the many freedmen who were moving about the country to come to Texas. This bill never reached the senate floor for a vote.

Many Texans were alarmed. They were afraid if Gaines had his way African-Americans would dominate the state. Newspapers printed harsh criticisms of Senator Gaines. One editor called him "an ignorant and arrogant ass" and "an uneducated cornfield Negro who accidentally got into a prominent State Office."[6]

Gaines continued to battle for racial integration. Displeased with public schools that separated Caucasian and African-American children, he urged parents to "send your children to any of the free schools you want to; go and attend yourselves, and see who puts them out; let me know who tries it!"

In the late summer of 1871, at the peak of his political career, Matt Gaines was a powerful influence among African-Americans. He was not afraid to fight for what he believed; and he refused to be politically controlled. Major political forces now feared him greatly.

A fight to have African-Americans appointed to more and better political offices brought Texas Governor Edmund Davis to the area. Not only was the governor unable to calm things down, but Matt made the most fiery speech of his career. On the senate floor, he accused his political opponents of being "as dishonest as they are powerful." He said Governor Davis and his "corrupt ring" had "set themselves up as BIG GODS of the Negroes" and they expected "worship, offices, money and power . . . while deep . . . in their hearts they despise us!"

He charged that because he was true to himself and his constituents and "refused to accept the Governor as God, he was to be read out of the party."[7] Apparently, he was right. After this speech, Gaines was exiled from his political party.

Democrats in his home district moved against Gaines through the courts. On December 9, 1871, the senator was indicted by the La Grange grand jury on the charge of bigamy. Released on $1,000 bail, his case was set for the following May. Matt Gaines filed many petitions to have his case transferred to federal court, charging his civil rights were being denied. The petitions were rejected, and his case came to trial July 15, 1873.

A jury of eleven Caucasians and one African-American heard testimony that Gaines married Fanny Sutton in 1867, and, without a divorce, had married Elizabeth Harrison in 1870. Several witnesses, including the minister who performed the first marriage ceremony, testified that the first marriage was considered illegally performed. Nevertheless, Gaines was found guilty, sentenced to a year at hard labor in the state penitentiary, and held in Fayette County Jail waiting for the result of his appeal.

Local newspapers were overjoyed by the senator's conviction. On July 15, 1873, the *Fayette County New Era* declared that Gaines' career in the senate was finished, adding that the next seat the senator would occupy would be in the Huntsville prison. The Brenham *Banner* of August 2, 1873 crowed, ". . . the late so-called Negro senator from Washington County . . . is now enjoying the hospitalities of the Sheriff of Fayette County, where he is detained as a convict."

However, Gaines remained popular with his constituency. All during the time he was embroiled in legal hearings, petitions, trials and appeals defending himself against the bigamy charge, he continued to function as a senator, fighting for the rights of the people who had elected him.

In November of 1873, the Texas Supreme Court overruled the decision of the district court and reprimanded the judge of the district court for denying Gaines' petition for transfer to a federal court. In spite of the final decision which fully cleared Matt Gaines of the charge against him, the press continued to call him a convicted felon who had gotten out of serving his sentence.

The July Brenham *Banner* of April 23, 1875 commented, "Matt belongs . . . in the state penitentiary. He is under conviction for felony, and a sentence to hard labor. . . . Why is so notorious a convict . . . allowed to run at large?"

Four months after the decision that freed him, Gaines was reelected to the senate. He won the election over Seth Shepard, a white candidate of the Democratic Party. Shepard challenged Gaines' seat saying he was a convicted felon and not eligible for the office.

J. E. Dillard, a longtime political enemy of Matt, was chairman of the senate committee on elections which handled the dispute. Gaines was not permitted to testify before the committee, and on March 25, 1874, Dillard pronounced Gaines ineligible, and recommended that Shepard be seated. Without connections to fight the decision, the political career of Matthew Gaines was over.

Gaines was in his early thirties when he was denied his senate seat. For the next twenty-six years little was heard of him. He returned to being a country preacher. And he taught Sunday school. The children he taught said he constantly told them of their dignity as a race.

On June 11, 1900, Matthew Gaines died. It was said he had predicted his death two months earlier. He was buried a few miles east of Giddings, Texas, in an unmarked grave.

Few people today know the story of Matt Gaines, who tried so hard to lead Texas into a bright future before most people in the state shared his ideals. But even though he was railroaded out of office and made powerless to continue his work, Matt Gaines is important in American history because of his far-sighted vision.

During a time when many Black lawmakers were proposing measures for the relief of their former masters, Gaines was working to prevent Black voters from being forced into voting a certain way. Most Black legislators accepted the control of their political parties, but Gaines was guided by the needs of his people.

When other politicians were satisfied with segregated schools, Gaines saw the error of segregation and cried out for the rights of children to be educated without being segregated. Early on, Gaines saw the value of Black power. He urged African-Americans to use their votes to obtain political independence and to influence issues.

Like most of his fellow Black legislators, Gaines was honest. But unlike most of them, he didn't mind making noise when he thought it would help to advance his cause. He cared less than most of them did about "looking respectable." Sometimes when he was strongly vocal, his colleagues were ashamed of him.

It is true that Matthew Gaines occasionally embarrassed the men of his day. Even now, his name is often left out of history books. But when one reads the debates of the Twelfth Legislature in which he served, the voice of Matthew Gaines comes alive. His words flash across generations. They shed light on the new day he saw coming when others could not see it — a day that he worked hard to bring about.

Barbara Jordan

Stateswoman and "Golden Orator"

BARBARA JORDAN's eyes gleamed with pride as she watched children performing at Barbara Jordan Elementary School in Austin, Texas. She was the guest of honor for the dedication program at this school that had been named for her. Scrubbed and dressed to shining perfection, the youngsters were doing their best to impress her, and they were succeeding.

They had helped roll out a red carpet for her, taken part in a ribbon-cutting ceremony, and listened respectfully while grown-ups spoke of hard work and dreams that had led to this joyful day. Now the students were making speeches they had written and singing songs they had composed. They recited poems they had created, and chanted an original rap. Earlier, Principal Kay Fowler had said that unlike most schools, named for historical people who had died, this school was named for a living historical person whom the students could see and touch, admire and emulate.

Barbara Jordan was deeply moved. When it was her turn to speak, she breathed deeply, her heart full to bursting, and said, "In case any of you wonder, it doesn't get any better than this!"[1]

Barbara Jordan's name first flashed around the world at the height of the 1976 Democratic Convention. She had gained the attention of the nation when she became the first African-American congresswoman from Texas. Among people who had heard her speak in public, she was known for her golden oratory. Because she was such a great speaker, she was chosen to give the keynote address for the Democratic Convention even though she was not well known throughout the country. Her speech was broadcast and televised nationally. And millions of people were spellbound by what this congresswoman was saying, by how she said it, and by her commanding presence.

"I feel . . . notwithstanding the past, that my presence

61

Barbara Jordan (1936–1996)
— Institute of Texan Cultures, San Antonio, Texas

here is one additional bit of evidence that the American Dream need not forever be deferred," she said. While she was speaking, viewers and listeners soared to heights seldom reached. They were responding to the earnest expression on her face, the magic, music, and rhythm of her voice, the depth of her thought, and the sincerity, logic, and spiritual quality of her ideas.

One reviewer wrote, "The audience was hers, she was the speech, and the message was hers alone. No one else could have delivered it."

Much of the world stood still and listened while she spoke. Then, countless people in the nation and around the world who had not known her before asked the question, "Who is Barbara Jordan?"

She was born Barbara Charline Jordan on February 21, 1936. Her parents were Ben and Arlyne Jordan. The family lived in a poor neighborhood of Houston, Texas, and Barbara was the youngest of three daughters. While she was growing up, she was a favorite of her mother's father, "Grandpa Patten." He was a junk dealer, and when Barbara was five, he made her his special helper and paid her a salary.

When she entered school, her father let it be known that he expected her to be an excellent student. Speaking of Barbara, he once said, "I realized when she was a little girl that Barbara was one of the rare ones. She was unhappy if she made less than a straight-A average in school."[2] Because he knew she had rare qualities and expected a great deal of herself, he held her to extremely high standards.

"I would come home with five A's and a B, and my father would say, 'Why do you have a B'?" Barbara recalled.[3]

"We knew from the very beginning she would do something different from the rest of us," Mary Justice York, a third-grade classmate, said of Barbara. "She was always the leader."[4]

When Barbara was about ten, she sometimes visited her older sister, Rose Mary, at Prairie View A&M College, where Rose Mary was a music student. "Even at that age, she was an unusual child," said Dr. Beulah Agnes Curry Jones, also a Prairie View music student at that time. "She had so much self confidence, and she was so charismatic, that if you met her once, you wanted to meet her again," Dr. Jones observed.

"The five to ten years difference in age between her and the college students didn't matter. We would go where she was. We liked to hear her ask questions. She didn't ask the 'how' or 'why' questions you would expect from a ten-year-old. She asked in-depth questions. For instance, she might ask, *After you finish reading that chapter, what are you going to do with what you learn from it?* '"[5]

Barbara lived up to the high standards her dad set for her and earned the high grades he expected her to earn. In fact, she achieved even more than he had asked. Fellow students elected her president of the Honor Society of her high school.

Her growing-up years were soured, however, by racial segregation which was openly advocated and enforced during that time in Houston and most of the United States. Hateful "white" and "colored" signs confronted her constantly on entrances to Houston buildings, city buses, public water fountains, and restrooms.

She often wondered: How could this ugly racial practice be changed? Could she do something to help bring about a change? Then one day Edith Sansom, an African-American attorney, spoke to Barbara Jordan's tenth-grade class. Attorney Sansom told the students that major changes could be made through politics. Barbara was challenged and inspired by the attorney's presentation. Edith Sansom was a woman, an African-American, and a lawyer pointing the way to progress through politics. Could this be the way she, Barbara Jordan, could work to bring about the changes so desperately needed? For the first time, she began to think about entering the powerful field of politics.

To prepare herself, she became a political science student at Texas Southern University. There she distinguished herself as a skilled speaker and debate artist. She was the only woman on a debate team that defeated debating teams from world-famous institutions, including Harvard University. After graduating with honors,[6] she entered Boston University Law School and earned an LL.B. degree in 1959. By 1960 she had begun to practice law from her home.

Twice during the early 1960s she ran unsuccessfully for the Texas House of Representatives. Then, in 1966, Barbara

Jordan became the first African-American elected to the Texas Senate since 1883. In addition, she was the first Aframerican woman to serve in the Texas Senate.

She was voted the outstanding freshman legislator by her colleagues in the senate. She also became the first freshman senator ever appointed to the Texas Legislative Council, the research branch of the legislature. Voters were so pleased with her work that they reelected her in 1968. In March 1972, she was elected president pro tempore of the senate. And on June 19, 1972, she was named Governor for a Day, becoming the first Aframerican to preside over a state legislative house.

All the while she was receiving public awards and recognition, Senator Jordan was working to achieve her goals. She sponsored a Texas Fair Employment Practices Committee, helped obtain the first increase in worker's compensation benefits in twelve years, and introduced the state's first minimum wage law. She sponsored bills to expand the Voting Rights Act of 1965 and to guarantee consumers fair pricing. She also introduced a bill to provide Social Security benefits for homemakers, but this bill failed to pass.

Barbara Jordan decided not to seek reelection in 1978. She said the decision had nothing to do with difficulties in mobility she was experiencing as the result of an old knee injury. She accepted a professorship at the Lyndon B. Johnson School of Public Affairs of the University of Texas at Austin. There her classes became so popular that students were sometimes selected by lottery.

Barbara Jordan was awarded twenty-nine honorary doctorate degrees from institutions that include Harvard University and Notre Dame University. She was elected to the Texas Women's Hall of Fame, named "Texan of the Year" for 1992, and voted "Best Living Orator" by the International Platform Association. She received the Harry S. Truman Public Service Award and the Eleanor Roosevelt Humanities Award; and she was selected by *World Almanac* for twelve consecutive years as one of the "Twenty-five Most Influential Women in America." In 1994, she was awarded the American Medal of Freedom by President Bill Clinton.

How does receiving so many awards and tributes from

world-famous people and organizations compare with being honored by students in elementary school? During the dedication ceremony for Barbara Jordan Elementary School, a girl walked up and embraced Barbara Jordan. She was very much like Barbara Jordan herself had been as a girl in fifth grade. Barbara's face beamed with warm love and pride.

At the age of fifty-nine, following a long illness, Barbara Jordan died January 17, 1996. The entire country mourned the loss of this great stateswoman who had overcome forbidding drawbacks and carved a wide, bright path of achievement for others to follow.

George T. "Mickey" Leland
Warrior Against World Hunger

On a dark, foggy day in August 1989, moisture drizzled down the windows of a small plane flying U.S. Congressman GEORGE T. "MICKEY" LELAND and fifteen others on a mission to relieve hunger in Ethiopia. Straining to see through fog and drizzle, the pilot couldn't make out land shapes below or cloud forms around him.

The pilot and his passengers felt tense, but the twin engines of the aircraft were humming smoothly. Suddenly, a steep mountain slope was directly in front of them, too close for the pilot to turn away. The airplane crashed into the side of the mountain and splintered into pieces.

Congressman Leland was chairman of the House Select Committee on World Hunger. He had created the committee himself because he was concerned about people around the world who did not have enough food to keep their bodies healthy, or, sometimes, even to keep themselves alive. This was his sixth mission to relieve hunger in East Africa, where famine was raging.

Days after the crash, the charred, crumpled wreck of the

plane was sighted on the side of an Ethiopian mountain. It was only seventy-five miles from the refugee camp the congressman had set out to visit six days earlier. Thick with trees and bushes, the terrain was dangerous and difficult to reach. Medical teams were lowered from helicopters to the wreck, but they found no survivors.

The world then learned that Mickey Leland had died as he had lived, trying to put an end to hunger on earth. As the United States grieved for this beloved fallen son, flags were lowered to half staff at the White House and on government buildings in Washington, in Texas, and in other parts of the country. Mickey Leland was a forty-four-year-old Texan who had spent ten years in Congress. In that time he had become one of the nation's best known and best loved congressional representatives.

But it had not always been that way. When Representative Leland was first elected to the Texas legislature in 1972, the other very proper state representatives in their very proper suits found it hard to believe their eyes. The new representative from Houston's Fifth District wore a brilliant African dashiki, and platform shoes. He also carried a leather shoulder bag. His flaming, crinkly red hair fanned out in a "mile-high" afro hairstyle, surrounding golden-cream colored skin, bright blue eyes, and a goatee.

As if that were not enough, the Honorable Representative Mickey Leland pulled little boy stunts! Once he squirted a water pistol at the vacant chair of the Speaker of the House. Another time he wound up a toy monkey and kept it bouncing on his desk. This was his way of showing the other representatives he thought they were voting like monkeys about an important issue.

His tricks made some people laugh. Others were disturbed. But Mickey Leland was not trying to be funny. Nor was he trying to be bizarre. He was showing his frustration.

He had been elected by the poorest district in Houston, which was also the poorest district in Texas. However, as he struggled to make laws to uplift the people he represented, he was opposed or ignored by most of the Texas legislature. He then resorted to the ways of a street fighter to call attention to

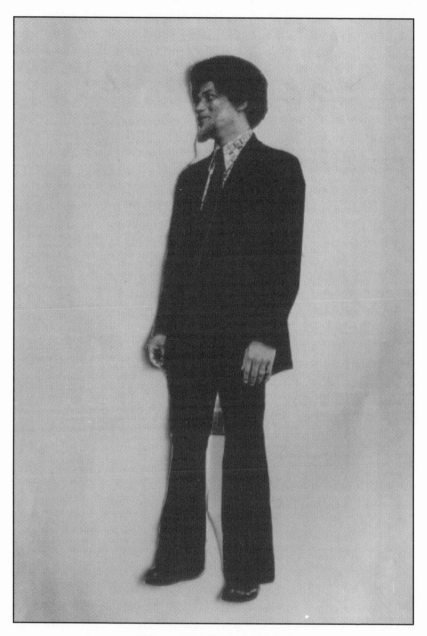

George T. "Mickey" Leland

the need for the lawmakers to act on behalf of the deprived people in his district.

At the low point of his helpless feelings, he decided the situation was hopeless and packed his bags to go home. However, other African-American representatives talked him out of leaving. In the end, his decision to remain in government became a blessing to starving people around the world.

Shortly after Mickey Leland was elected to the Texas House of Representatives, he visited Africa for the first time as a representative of the United States government. The country he visited was Tanzania, and he planned to stay for three weeks. Instead, he remained in Tanzania three months. He was so caught up in what he was doing that he did not call home to tell his family he had decided to stay longer than he had planned.

"I got lost in Africa," he told *SEEDS*, a magazine published by an organization that fights hunger. "Nobody knew where I was. My mother thought I was dead. But the fact is, I got totally absorbed in Africa."[1]

The congressman's mother, Alice Rains, was very close to her son. She had supported him through many phases of his life, and he made it a point to keep in touch with her. "My mother was the driving force in my life," Congressman Leland often said. "She got through a lot of obstacles, and she made it."

His visit to Tanzania was followed by many journeys to the African continent. During these visits, he worked with the people, learning from them and about them. As a result, Congressman Leland became a U.S. international ambassador with the mission of ending hunger around the world.

Speaking of his determination to end hunger, the congressman often recalled visiting the Sudan in 1984 and seeing a small girl die. Afterwards he described what happened: "The child looked about seventy or eighty years old, a skeleton of a person, with a thin layer of brown skin . . . [she] had just a faint breath of life in her." According to Congressman Leland, he turned to a worker standing next to him to ask about the girl, and when he looked at her again, she had stopped breathing. "While I was talking to him, she died," he said. "I can see her face right now. Every day I see her face."[2]

Congressman Leland was elected to the United States Congress in 1978. He filled the seat left by Congresswoman Barbara Jordan when she retired. By this time he was wearing expensive, European-cut business suits, and he no longer found it necessary to play street games to make a point. But he remained a strong warrior for worthy causes.

One of the first programs he sponsored sent African-American teenagers from Houston to Israel to learn about Jewish culture and heritage. The visit helped lessen the gap between African-Americans and Jewish-Americans who were not getting along with each other very well at that time.

Once, the congressman himself rode a bicycle through Israel. Although he was a Roman Catholic, as he bicycled through Israel he often quoted from the Talmud, "If you save one life, you save the whole world."

In addition to visiting Africa and Israel, Congressman Leland visited Cuba, a country which was not on good terms with the United States. Even so, while he was in Cuba, he arranged for that country to release three political prisoners and their families. He also flew to Vietnam and returned with three children whose father had escaped from Vietnam and was living in Houston.

Twice he served as chairman of the Congressional Black Caucus. He also served as a member of a subcommittee on telecommunications. In this position, he scolded TV networks for not employing African-Americans in appropriate numbers for jobs on the air and positions off the air.

Not everyone liked the way Mickey Leland operated. Some people said he was too liberal. Others thought he should bring relief to hungry people in the United States before he tackled hunger in other countries.

After a visit to the Sudan he answered such critics by saying, "I am as much a citizen of this world as I am of my country. To hell with those people who are critical of what I am able to do to help save people's lives. I don't mean to sound hokey, but I grew up on a Christian ethic which says we are supposed to help the least of our brothers."

In his Houston district the congressman remained popular no matter what anyone outside the district said. He was re-elected to his congressional seat by overwhelming majorities five times. People who voted for him could depend upon his ongoing support of food programs for their district. They also knew that he never stopped working to obtain housing for homeless people in their district.

Congressman Leland was born in Lubbock, Texas, on November 27, 1944. He was named George Thomas Leland, but he never used the name he had been given at birth. Instead, he chose to be called "Mickey," a nickname his grandfather gave him.

Shortly after Mickey was born, his father abandoned the family. His mother, who was a short-order cook before the separation, became a teacher. She later moved the family to Houston into a large frame house her father had built in Houston's Fifth Ward.

During childhood, Mickey and his younger brother, Gaston, were sheltered from race problems. Everyone in their world was Black, and their mother never talked about race. But when he left the Black neighborhood to attend college, Mickey learned all about racial prejudice and bigotry. He also became aware of Dr. Martin Luther King, Jr., and the work he was doing. And he began to think of running for a political office.

During his days as a Texas Southern University student, he led marches, organized strikes, and made hot-headed speeches standing on the tables of the school cafeteria. His fiery behavior frightened many people, including some members of his family. His aunt pleaded with him to change. His grandmother didn't want him in her house. But his mother stood by him even though she was afraid for him.

"I never tried to stop him because I knew we [African-Americans] had been suppressed. Somebody had to make it happen," she said. "You didn't want it to be your child who was going to do this and yet you knew — somebody had to do it."[3]

She had good reason to worry. The congressman once admitted, "I was in a very militant mode at the time. I was very much dissatisfied with society, its injustice. I'm not so sure that I would not have been willing at the time to become violent."[4]

In 1970, Mickey Leland graduated from Texas Southern

University with a degree in pharmacy. Before he entered politics he worked for two years as a pharmacist and teacher.

After he became a congressman, he sometimes encouraged young people to follow his example and make a difference in the world. He also tried to inspire them to rise above anything or anyone trying to hold them down.

Once, standing on the steps of the U.S. Capitol Building, he told a group of young congressional summer interns: "When I had just graduated from high school in the 1960s, I joined the civil rights and the anti-war movement. I know I made a difference!

"They said I'd never graduate from college. Well, I graduated from college. I got a degree in pharmacy, and I got elected a member of Congress. So what greater testimony could there be?"[5]

In 1984, Congressman Leland married Allison Walton, an investment banker. When he died, the couple had a three-year-old son, Jarret-David, and Mrs. Leland was pregnant. In January of 1990 she prematurely gave birth to twin sons.

President George Bush, who was in office when the congressman died, said of him: "I have known, admired and worked with Mickey Leland for many years. His sense of compassion and desire to help those in need has aided millions of people from Houston to Addis Ababa."[6]

Writing about Congressman Leland in the *Houston Chronicle*, newspaper columnist Jane Ely penned words that could well be his epitaph: ". . . he was a person of magnificent, infinite hope. He simply believed hunger could be ended, the world could be bettered, and all of humanity could rise to its best."[7]

Angela Shelf Medearis
Author of Children's Books

ANGELA SHELF MEDEARIS is lots of fun! So, naturally, she writes books that are fun to read. One of her stories is called "We Eat Dinner in the Bathtub." It is about a family that eats in the bathtub, cooks in the bedroom, and parks the car in the kitchen. Oh, and their dog sleeps in the refrigerator!

"It's just a silly story that makes the kids laugh," Medearis said. But all the while the children are laughing, the story is teaching them a great deal about order.

Where does she get ideas for stories? "If they're weird — something really crazy — I say they come from eating too much chocolate in the morning," she teased. Then she joked that ideas for a "normal" story come when she hasn't eaten enough chocolate! "I just love chocolate!" she laughed.

Born in Hampton, Virginia, in 1956, Angela lived in many places as a child. Her father was in the air force, and the family moved around as he changed duty stations. "We came to Texas when I was fifteen," she recalled. "I've been here longer than anywhere else." Medearis now lives in Austin and declares she will be a Texan forever.

Angela's dream of becoming a professional author wasn't realized right away. She began writing stories when she was a little girl and continued to write as a young woman. But she didn't know how to become a professional writer.

For a long time she worked in offices, even though she detested office work. "I hated it," she said. "You should never work any place where you hate the work. And the very thought of putting on hose and sitting behind a desk from nine to five for thirty years blew my mind!"

Even so, Angela did her clerical jobs well. But because her heart was not in her work, time after time she was "let go" from positions she held. Then, in her words, "In 1987 I got fired from yet another job as a legal secretary." This time she was given three months' pay.

Angela Shelf Medearis

For the first time she could afford to stay home and write instead of having to find another job. She was delighted. "I said, 'If I sell something, this is meant to be.'"

One day, a magazine about water beds brought a story from her, and she was on her way! After that, all of her jobs were related to writing or publishing.

One time she handled publicity for a cartoonist. At another time she wrote vignettes for the Texas State Historical Association. Later, working for *Texas Monthly* magazine, she learned the writing and publishing business. Hired part-time to pack, weigh, and ship books, she worked her way up to become assistant editor.

While she earned a living through various jobs, Angela was honing her skills as an author. She praises her family for their support during those days. The long, hard struggle to success would have been even harder without their help, she says.

"When I said I was going to be a writer, it was like saying I was going to be a brain surgeon," she laughed. "Nobody in the family had ever done that." However, she is proud of her parents and siblings, her daughter and husband: "They all supported me every step of the way!"

It was during this time that she founded Book Boosters to improve reading skills of elementary school students. Medearis began Book Boosters in one school with a $50 donation. There were 120 students, and she was the only tutor. Now, five years later, the program services five schools and about 200 students. There are five tutors, and contributions top $30,000.

Tutors work with second- and third-grade students. "We make everything fun," Medearis explained. "Sometimes we work outside and play games, even baseball. There may be 200 flash cards in a game, but you have to read them all to play. And the kids think of it as fun, not work!"

Once a newspaper reporter asked a third grader how she felt about being in Book Boosters. "Oh, I love it because I don't have to do any work. We just play!" the girl said. Asked to explain what she had done, the child said she had read a book, written stories about the characters, and written a book report! Medearis laughed heartily about the incident. "That little girl worked hard and called it fun. She also showed pride in her work and in herself!" Explaining that students who read poorly usually have poor opinions of themselves, she said, "We work with their self esteem, and it doesn't take long."

Teachers marvel at how quickly Book Boosters' students change, she observed. She tells a favorite story about a shy, silent boy. To the amazement of his teacher, after learning to read through Book Boosters, the boy became bold "overnight," constantly asking and answering questions in class.

While she was building Book Boosters, Angela continued to write children's stories. Time and again, editors rejected her stories, leaving her frustrated and disappointed. But she refused to give up. Instead, she studied suggestions made by editors, rewrote the stories, and mailed them out again.

At last, three years after she began seeking publication, it happened. A book Angela had written about her mother's family during the Great Depression was accepted by a publisher. She was ecstatic!

Picking Peas for a Penny, Angela's first book, was published in 1990. Now, four years later, more than thirty of her books are in print. How different her life is from the days of constant rejection letters! Today, publishers ask her to write stories for them. Also, schools, libraries and organizations around the country invite her to visit, tell her stories, and talk about how she writes them.

When Angela speaks, she keeps her listeners laughing, especially when she answers questions. "Since you do so much traveling, who keeps your house for you?" she is asked at times.

"Oh, there's this Black lady who comes in and cleans the house for me," the popular author answers cheerfully. Then she throws her arms up in the air, smiles, steps forward, and says, "And here she is!"

Afterward she explains that she enjoys housework. "When I was a little girl, every day I'd go through the Sears Roebuck catalogue and pick out furniture for my house after I got married. I still enjoy choosing furniture, cleaning, cooking, folding towels, and things like that."

Many children who want to follow in her footsteps ask at what age they should start writing. Her answer is always the same, "Start writing right away. You are never too young. We need young writers."

Children also ask, "Why do you like to write?" Her answer makes them giggle.

"Because when I wake up in the morning, I can roll out of bed and start working!" Declaring that she enjoys working in a house dress without having to don the hated hose, she says, "Writing is the only job I know where you can go to work in your underwear if you want to, and eat chocolate all day! Who would care?"

She also gets to make a home for her husband Michael, her daughter Deanna, and her granddaughter Anysa. For Angela, that is as much fun as writing. Further, she is happy to be surrounded by books she can read, and books she is writing.

A number of new books for children by Angela Medearis are being published as this cheerful, hard-working author moves toward a new goal. She has decided to write books for adults. At present she is working on two adult books, a cowboy story and a murder mystery. Small wonder that Angela's voice is compelling, her eyes are shining, and she is smiling broadly when she says, "Writing is a great job!"

Doris ("Dorie") Miller
Pearl Harbor Hero

December 7, 1941. The U.S. battleship *West Virginia* was pitching and rolling in the calm waters of Pearl Harbor in the early hours of a clear, beautiful, lazy Sunday. Below the main deck, navy enlisted man DORIS MILLER was methodically collecting laundry. He was so used to the motion of the ship in the water that he was not aware of it. His body was steady, his footsteps firm and sure.

His job was not challenging. Miller knew he was qualified to do far more than the job required, far more than he was

Doris ("Dorie") Miller

ever allowed to do. However, Doris Miller, often called "Dorie" Miller, was an African-American. And the navy enlisted African-Americans as cooks, stewards, or waiters, and nothing else. Black men were inducted into the U.S. Navy of 1941 to serve and clear tables in the junior officers' mess, shine shoes, and make beds.

African-American men were forbidden to practice with or fire any weapon. During combat, they were assigned to battle stations as ammunition handlers. Like millions of Black Americans of his time, in order to survive, Miller had to submit to doing less than he knew he could, and being less in the eyes of the world than he knew he was.

One of the few racially integrated activities aboard ship was boxing. And at 6'3, 225 pounds, Doris Miller was the heavyweight champion of the USS *West Virginia*. However, navy policy determined that aboard this battleship, his duties were to serve and clean up after white officers.

As a youth, Doris Miller had hunted squirrels with a .22 rifle and had become an excellent marksman. Before he joined the navy, he had considered becoming a taxidermist. During the year and a half before Pearl Harbor was bombed, Miller had twice attended secondary battery gunnery school aboard the USS *Nevada*. He had learned about weapons, but was not allowed to fire them.

Suddenly, the calm of the Sunday routine was shattered. Something was happening! But what? *Explosive noises. Bombs? Loud cries; guttural sounds; rushing footsteps; more explosions!* Miller dashed up ship ladders into a scene on the main deck that he would see in his mind time and again the rest of his short life.

Ship sirens wailed, cutting across the blaring voice that blasted through the loud speaker: "Man your battle stations! Man your battle stations!" Overhead the sky was specked with Japanese fighter planes circling, diving, and bombing the American ships in the harbor. On deck, the captain of the *West Virginia* lay fatally wounded. And the body of a gunner who had been killed lay beside an antiaircraft gun.

Dodging enemy bullets, Doris pulled the captain to safety. Then he sprinted to the dead sailor's gun. Over and over a thought rushed through his mind: *I can do it! I can do it! I know I can do it!* He had never been trained to use the weapon, but he was certain he knew what should be done.

Twenty-nine Japanese fighter planes were raining bombs on the ships. Taking his time, Doris Miller aimed carefully at one aircraft, then at another, and another. Over and over, he fired calmly, deliberately, and with precision at the Zero Fighter Planes swooping through the skies. When an aircraft fell into the ocean, he turned his gun and aimed at a plane in the air above. After about fifteen minutes, someone thundered the order, "Abandon ship!"

In his book *At Dawn We Slept,* Gordon Prange described the reaction of a *West Virginia* officer who watched Seaman Miller in action: ". . . Miller, who was not supposed to handle anything deadlier than a swab, [was] manning a machine gun, 'blazing away as though he had fired one all his life.' As he did so, his usually impassive face bore the deadly smile of a berserk Viking."[1]

According to navy records, Miller said about the event, "It wasn't hard. I just pulled the trigger, and she worked fine. I had watched others with these guns. I guess I fired her for about fifteen minutes. I think I got one of those planes. They were diving pretty close to us."

In fact, eyewitnesses said Miller downed more than one plane. Some say he shot down five airplanes; others agree there were four. Navy records credit the twenty-two-year-old sailor with shooting down two enemy aircraft.

For some time after the bombing of Pearl Harbor, reports in the American media told the story of an unnamed Black messman hero. However, it was not until March 14, 1942, that Doris Miller was revealed as the hero by the *Pittsburgh Courier,* an African-American newspaper. Almost overnight, his name became known throughout the country. To his mother's distress, Doris, the name she had given her son at birth, was changed to the more masculine name "Dorie" in newspaper and navy reports.

In recognition of his courage, Doris Miller was cited for bravery and decorated with the Silver Star on May 7, 1942. Nevertheless, he was not given a promotion nor transferred to duties appropriate for the ability he had shown. Instead, his face was pictured on a navy recruiting poster, and he was sent to Harlem to drum up support for U.S. War Bonds.

Miller went on to serve as a steward aboard the heavy cruiser *Indianapolis*. Later, he was assigned to the aircraft carrier escort USS *Liscome Bay*. On November 24, 1943, the ship was torpedoed and sunk by a Japanese submarine in the Pacific Ocean near the Gilbert Islands. Miller, twenty-four, still a mess attendant, was among 646 men who went down with the ship.

One year later, Doris Miller was presumed dead by the U.S. Navy. He was issued the Purple Heart and other honors posthumously. An auditorium in Austin, Texas, has been given the name of the Central Texas hero. In 1972, the USS *Doris Miller* was christened in his honor. The ship was a destroyer escort, designed to seek out and destroy enemy submarines. The 1.3 billion dollar vessel was decommissioned in 1991.

In 1984, Dr. Leroy Ramsey, a retired university history professor, decided to write a book on Black military men and women in World War II. An African-American veteran of that war, he had watched TV programs marking the fortieth anniversary of D-Day in Europe. These programs made him angry because so few Black Americans were included.

Ramsey reviewed the records of Black service persons who had received military honors and discovered that not one of 1.3 million Black Americans who served in World Wars I and II had received the Medal of Honor. He learned that the country had issued 3,417 Medal of Honor citations, the nation's highest award for military valor. Then he decided that instead of writing a book, he would dedicate his time to getting the Medal of Honor awarded to one or more veterans of the two world wars.

"The first thing that the Congressional Medal of Honor asks is [that] you have to go beyond the call of duty," Ramsey has said. "That phrase cannot be lost when it comes to Dorie Miller. Here was a man who did what he was not allowed to do. Just manning that machine gun was going beyond the call of duty right there."[2]

However, the secretary of the navy has objected to bills that were introduced in the U.S. House of Representatives and the U.S. Senate to present the Medal of Honor to Doris Miller.

Noting that Miller has had a ship named in his honor and has received the navy's second highest award, Ramsey said, "The opposition I've been running into with Miller is that if we want to give him a Congressional Medal of Honor too, we might as well give him the whole navy. People have said to me, 'Hasn't he received enough?'"[3] Race also continues to be a problem. "A Black guy has to do twice as much to get half as much," Ramsey observed.[4]

According to Ramsey, the Persian Gulf War and the death of U.S. Representative Mickey Leland of Houston sidetracked efforts to obtain the Medal of Honor for Miller. Nevertheless, Ramsey maintains confidence that the day will come when a Congressional Medal of Honor is issued for Seaman Doris Miller.

Quiet, soft-spoken, and intelligent, Doris Miller had been named after the midwife who attended his birth on a small farm near Waco, Texas, in 1919. It was a name he enjoyed having during his brief life. With or without the Congressional Medal of Honor, it is a name the world needs to remember with love, pride, and gratitude.

Bill Pickett
First Steer Wrestler/Creator of Bulldogging

On December 9, 1971, BILL PICKETT became the first African-American cowboy enshrined in the National Cowboy Hall of Fame in Oklahoma City. And well he should be. He was the best! He led all the rest!

The world knows his name because he initiated the sport of steer wrestling known as "bulldogging." In the 1800s, "when the West was wild," nobody wrestled steers, and there was no such thing as bulldogging. Until along came Bill Pickett.

Bill developed ways to recapture animals that broke away from a herd. Like other cowboys, he could catch runaways with his lasso, or gallop his horse beside a break-away animal and force it back into cattle lines. But if the brush was too thick for a lasso, or the brute was not near cattle lines, something else had to be done.

While other cowboys stared in disbelief, Pickett would leap from his galloping horse onto the head of a running steer. Digging his feet into the ground to bring the animal to a halt, Bill would twist the steer's head, forcing its nose and mouth up. He would then clamp his teeth into the beast's lip or nose, throwing his full weight onto the animal's lip or nostrils. The steer would lunge a time or two and flop over on its side. Then Pickett would throw both hands in the air. This was a signal to others that the steer was down and they could come to help.

Today steer wrestling is extremely popular in rodeo contests. Many cowboys say it is also the most difficult feat.

Bill was born in Williamson County, Texas, in 1863. His mother was a Native American of the Choctaw tribe. His father was a mixture of African, Native American, and Caucasian. Bill grew up on Texas ranches. As a youth he lived, rode, and roped with Mexican *vaqueros* (cowboys). He stood 5'9 tall with skinny legs and big hands. His arms and shoulders were as broad as a wrestler's. His body was as supple as a dancer's.

Bill Pickett and the beloved Spradley, his "war horse."

He first attracted the attention of his fellow cowboys by "tailing" a steer that suddenly dashed from the herd. Bill was riding Chico, his favorite horse. "I'll fetch him," he yelled.

Spinning Chico around, he galloped beside the escaping animal, grabbed its stiffened tail, and by sheer strength up-ended the beast. The steer hung in midair a moment, then crashed to the ground. It staggered to its feet, bellowing and shaking its head. Pickett then calmly led him back to the cattle lines.

Bill's steer wrestling began accidentally. One day an angry cow charged him. She was angry and weak from calving. Her horns were aimed at Chico. Pickett leaned down and grabbed a horn to keep Chico from being gored. He was jerked from the saddle and Chico scampered away. Pickett said later: "I held on tight. I knew if I let go, we'd have a foot race. And I never was fast on my feet. I got my left arm under the other horn and twisted her nose toward the sky, forcing her neck back to bust her down. I sure was mad at that darned cow for trying to hurt my Chico!"

Meantime, Chico galloped into an area where cowhands were gathered. When the horse arrived agitated and rider-less, the men were alarmed. At once, some of them rode out to look for Bill.

Pickett was wrestling the enraged cow, and his strength was giving out. Suddenly, he remembered how his bulldog, Spike, subdued steers, and he sank his teeth into the cow's upper lip just as Spike would have done. The longhorn cow came crashing down.

Afterward, Bill described what happened:

"That's how the boys found me — arms locked over both horns and still biting the cow's muzzle with my teeth. The boss rode up and remarked, 'Bill, you're holding that cow like a bulldog.' He throwed his rope, and I put it around her head. 'Turn her loose, Bill,' he said. 'She can't get you now.'

"Well, she got up and charged me. But the rope stopped her. Then the boys went to work with their ropes, and they soon had her and the calf out of the mesquite.

"It was while riding back to the herd that I got the idea of jumping from my horse to cattle's head and horns, catching and throwing them with my teeth like old Spike, as it wouldn't cut up the stock like that bulldog did."

In time, bulldogging became a sport for Pickett. He was recruited by Joe, Zack, and George Miller, brothers who owned the famous 101 Ranch in Oklahoma. Sponsored by the Millers at shows around the country, Bill befriended and performed with legendary cowboys including Tom Mix and Will Rogers. Even so, it was Bill Pickett the newspapers lauded as "the most daring cowboy alive, 'The Dusky Demon.'"

Boasting that Pickett could even overcome a Mexican bull, Joe Miller put an ad in a Mexican newspaper challenging any *two* bullfighters to throw *one* steer while Bill Pickett was throwing *three!* When the challenge was not accepted, Joe accused the bullfighters of "showing the white feather." Then, without consulting Bill, he announced that Pickett, unassisted, would spend five minutes on the head of the most blood-hungry bull Mexico could provide!

Ring officials, bullfighters and their fans were dumbfounded. A Mexican matador never dared to touch an animal. He took pride in stepping aside to avoid a mad bull rushing toward him. Also, the necks of these bulls were too thick to be twisted down. If Miller thought his cowboy could master such a bull bare handed, he was a fool! Sick of Joe Miller's bragging, they eagerly covered the bet. They were certain the bull — if Pickett could touch him — would shake him off in seconds and gore him to death.

Señor Rivero, manager of Plaza del Toro (Bull's Plaza) in Mexico City, agreed to hold the contest there. For the encounter, he chose Chiquita Frijole (Little Bean), a purple bull with bean-sized speckles. Beautiful and blood thirsty, he had killed two men and six horses. Ordinarily he would have been put to death. But crowds of spectators had saved him by shouting that such a magnificent bull should not be killed. So, he remained alive — bellowing and pawing the ground, horns set for hooking, longing to kill again.

"Think you can handle him, Bill?" Joe asked.

"Like you said, Colonel Joe, they ain't growed a beast these old hands can't hold," Pickett replied, holding up hands that looked like chiseled, black steel.

However, that night Bill came to Joe's tent and stood quietly. "You change your mind, Bill?" Joe asked.

"No, sir. I ain't afraid of that little old specklety bull. It's just that a man's time has got to come sooner or later. . . . Maybe this is my time, maybe it ain't. But if'n it is, I wants to know if I can be put away amongst my friends."

"We'll bury you on the 101," said Joe.

"In the hard ground, where the coyotes can't scratch out my bones?"

"In the hard ground, Bill." Joe Miller agreed.

Pickett left the tent smiling.

Next day, thousands of people from all walks of life streamed to Plaza del Toro. Even Mexico's president, Porfirio Díaz, was there. The crowd wanted Pickett to lose. Their raucous voices wildly cheered the bull. Then something happened so ugly it was hard to believe. Several bullfighters walked into the ring carrying a black coffin. Printed on the coffin was *"El PINCHARINO"* (a man who has been riddled by a bull's horns). *"El Pincharino! El Pincharino!"* the crowd screamed gleefully.

A lesser man might have lost courage. But Bill Pickett was confident and eager for battle as he entered the ring with a show troupe of fourteen hundred. He was riding Spradley, the pony that had been his constant ride since he retired Chico.

Stopping before President Díaz, Pickett reared Spradley in a courteous salute. The crowd booed and hissed. Sickening noises were coming from Little Bean's chute, where he was being stabbed with sharp instruments to make him angry. A bundle of fireworks exploded. Then Chiquita Frijole lunged into the arena looking for his tormentors, his hide scorched and bloody.

He spotted Pickett, then lurched around and charged, horns lowered for the kill. The crowd went wild! Their beloved Chiquita Frijole was about to show those bragging Americans who was boss! With the bull's horns seconds from plunging into his body, Spradley jumped aside and kicked his hind hoofs into Little Bean's ribs.

The bull slid several yards, raising a fire storm of dust and grit. He spun around, charged again, and rammed his horns deep into Spradley's rump. With a screaming whinny Spradley sank to the ground, blood spurting from his hide. Little Bean yanked his horns out to strike again.

Like lightning, Pickett landed between the blood-smeared horns on Little Bean's head and grasped his neck. The crowd roared! This cowboy who expected to stay on Chiquita Frijole's head for five minutes could be smashed to the ground with one head toss!

The bull swung his head from side to side, swinging the cowboy like a whip, trying to throw him off. He slammed Bill into a wall. He rammed his head against the ground, trying to break Pickett's grip.

One — two — three minutes passed. Bill regained a head hold. With one arm around each horn, his huge hands squeezed the throat. His powerful knees pinched the animal's nostrils shut so he couldn't breathe. Bill seemed glued to Little Bean's head. Another three minutes passed and the bull was tottering. Bill's five minutes were up, and his strength was leaving him. But the Mexican timekeeper did not stop the clock.

Somebody hurled a sharp stone which sliced Bill's face, and blood ran down his cheeks. The angry crowd howled insults at him and shouted, *"Viva el Toro!"* (Long live the bull!) Knives, bottles, fruits, canes, and a cushion rained on Bill Pickett. Hate was running wild, and no one stopped it.

Their hats wet with spit that came from the crowd above them, the show troupe appealed to the police. But the police only laughed at them. They pleaded with Joe Miller, but he was afraid to do anything. Ten minutes passed, twelve, fifteen. Still Bill held on, his face gray, his eyes filled with tears.

At last, Miller spoke to Ves Pegg, a cowboy standing beside him. "Them bastards ain't going to ring that bell, Ves. They aim to let that bull kill old Bill. Strip off your shirt. Now the moment Bill lets go, get over that wall. Wave your garment as close to the bull as you dare, and see if you can save your comrade's life!"

Just then, a brick struck Pickett in the side, cracking two of his ribs. Bill groaned and slipped off the bull. Chiquita Frijole lowered his head and pointed his horns for the death thrust just as Ves Pegg, half naked, leaped over the barrier. To the astonishment of both bull and spectators, he was waving his shirt almost in the bull's face. Little Bean hesitated, then jumped over Pickett and charged Ves Pegg.

Pegg leaped over the wall and Bill staggered to safety. He returned to salute President Díaz as more knives, bricks, and bottles came hurling down. But Bill led his crippled pony from the arena with quiet dignity.

Then the crowd swarmed down to reach Pickett and the show troupe, yelling, "Kill the Black man! Kill all the American dogs!" However, fearing trouble, Díaz had troops ready, and he commanded them to protect the Americans from the murderous crowd.

That night, Mexico City was restless, but the hatred shown the Americans did not last. The story of what happened to Bill in Mexico attracted kings, queens, and common folk from around the world to Ranch 101, where they hoped to see Bill Pickett.

In time, bulldogging became unfashionable. It was banned in many places as "cruelty to dumb animals." More than once Pickett was arrested and fined. By the early 1920s the sport had become steer wrestling.

Bill was growing old. Many of his bones had been broken, and he had lost his front teeth from biting steers. He obtained a ranch in Oklahoma. But after his wife died and his children married, he missed his former life. In 1932, he returned to Ranch 101. Zack Miller was sick, his brothers dead. The poorly kept property was in financial trouble, and an auction was planned.

Zack owned some horses that he did not want auctioned off, and Bill agreed to take them from the herd. But one horse kept moving back to a corner of the corral. Pickett roped the horse, then pulled the rope hand over hand, hauling the animal toward him.

Snorting and rearing, the horse chopped at the cowboy with his forefeet. Pickett jumped back, but not in time. The hammer blows of the hoofs struck his head and chest. On April 2, 1932, eleven days after the horse pawed him, Bill Pickett died. As Joe Miller had promised, Bill was buried in the hard ground on Ranch 101.

Phylicia Rashad
Singer, Dancer, World-famous Actress

The long, sleek, open-top limousine crawled along the street. It was part of the Thanksgiving Day parade given by Macy's department store in New York. Inside the car a long, sleek, gorgeous African-American woman sat so she could see the crowds thronging the sidewalks and they could see her. Looking from one side of the street to the other, she smiled and waved at the hordes of people. The crowd went wild.

"There she is!"

"That's Claire Huxtable, Bill Cosby's wife!"

"*Oooooooo,* look! She's even prettier than she is on TV!"

"Hi, Claire!"

"We love you, Claire!"

They shouted, laughed, waved and threw kisses. Now the young woman stood up, smiling and waving at her adoring fans as they called to her. The holiday spirit was in the air, and she was having a wonderful time. But a quick glance at her watch told her she would have to hurry when the parade ended or she would miss a very important appointment.

She was not Claire Huxtable. Not *really.* Her name was PHYLICIA RASHAD, and she was an actress. But many people thought of her as Claire Huxtable, the character she played on *The Cosby Show.* The tremendously popular television show was watched by people around the world.

The Cosby Show broadcast interesting, funny stories about an African-American family facing real life problems. The famous comedian Bill Cosby played the role of the father, who was a doctor. His wife, Claire, was a smart, pretty lawyer. As their children got into all kinds of scrapes and sometimes more serious problems, Claire always knew the right thing to say or do to keep her family safe and smiling.

For many broadcast seasons, the show was on TV every week, not only in the U.S. but also in other countries. Time and again it was rated the most watched television show in America. Phylicia had been a well-known actress before she joined the cast of *The Cosby Show*. However, as a result of her artistry in portraying Claire Huxtable, she became one of the most famous actresses in the world.

Explaining that being on *The Cosby Show* was rewarding in unexpected ways, the talented actress said: "Most families have a lot of love in them, and people enjoy seeing that reflected on television. I've even had women come up to me and tell me, 'Honey, you don't know how many marriages you've saved.' One woman said that her daughter and son-in-law were about to break up, but watching the show they started to reconsider and take a little bit more time to enjoy each other, to talk and to communicate and not get so annoyed by little things."[1]

When the parade was over, Phylicia went straight to the main offices of Macy's store to watch the football pre-game TV show that sportscaster Ahmad Rashad was hosting. He had told her to be sure to watch the program because he was going to do a special feature that he wanted her to see.

Bill Cosby had introduced Ahmad to Phylicia in an off-handed way one day on the set of *The Cosby Show*. Since then, the two had become fast friends. Phylicia wondered what the feature would be about. Whatever Ahmad had planned for this particular show would be outstanding because forty million fans were tuned in for the Thanksgiving Day football game. And indeed it was an excellent feature. Her heart swelled with pride as she sat watching him.

However, when the feature was over, Ahmad kept talking. A startled Phylicia jumped up, her body tense, her eyes glued to the TV set. *She could hardly believe her ears . . . He was talking to her! But what was he saying?* "Phylicia, will you marry me?" Ahmad Rashad's clear voice came from the television set to Phylicia and forty million football fans! Phylicia was shocked — and delighted. For a moment she stood rock-still, unable to move. Then she moved. *Fast!*

The young actress raced over to NBC studios where Rashad was broadcasting. She wanted to get there in time to sit in his chair at the game's half-time and give her answer. And she made it.

Forty million viewers heard her happily say "yes."

"I'm never gonna live that down," she laughed afterward.

Phylicia Rashad

"I loved it, and I almost missed seeing it."[2] They were married a few weeks after millions of people had watched them get engaged.

The time came when she asked Ahmad how he would have handled the situation if she had said no. He said if that had happened, he would have said, "Well, I was just kidding, I don't even know the girl!"[3]

Phylicia was born in Houston, Texas, in 1948. Her father was Andrew Allen, a dentist. Her mother, Vivian Ayers Allen, was a celebrated poet, known as Vivian Ayers (featured earlier in this book). Her sister, Debbie, was born in 1950 (also featured earlier). Like Phylicia, she became a superstar actress, singer, and dancer. Their brother, Andrew "Tex" Allen, became a well-known jazz composer and musician.

When Phylicia was nine years old, her parents separated. But her father continued to be an important part of the family until his death in 1984. In fact, according to Phylicia, the Allen family was much like her TV family, the Huxtables. The two families had different environments, however. The Allens lived in Houston surrounded by trees, grass, sky and sun, enjoying what Phylicia calls "a rich and lush life."[4] The Huxtables also lived well, but they were New Yorkers, surrounded by cement streets and brick buildings.

Nevertheless, comparing the two families while *The Cosby Show* was still being aired, Phylicia once said, "The kids are just as crazy, the mother's just as smooth. That energy is the same, and that love is the same."[5] Although her dad was a "life of the party," fun-loving person, he stopped laughing if one of his children received poor grades, and grounded that child until class marks were acceptable.

When Phylicia was thirteen years old, her mother walked into the house and made a surprising announcement. "I've had enough of this environment!" she said. That was the beginning of an exciting family sojourn to Mexico about which Phylicia said, "We packed up everything, got on the Greyhound bus and headed for Mexico City. It changed our perspective on life because we'd never been out of the country. The experience made us fearless and independent."[6] By the time the family returned to Houston many months later,

93

Phylicia had learned to speak Spanish well. Back home again, she studied drama and joined a choir. Then she enrolled at Howard University. Phylicia, who had always been a good student, was graduated from Howard with high honors. Then she moved to New York. Later, following in her big sister's footsteps, Debbie went to Howard, became an honor graduate, and joined Phylicia in New York.

Success did not come to either sister immediately. But they had studied and prepared themselves well, and they were ready for every opportunity that came their way. Each of them could sing, dance, and act. Vivian Ayers said of her daughters, "Phylicia learned to dance, and Debbie learned to sing, but I think Phylicia was *born* to sing, and Debbie was *born* to dance."[7]

According to Debbie, when they were children, Phylicia did not recognize her own beauty. "Growing up, she always thought she was an ugly duckling," Debbie said of Phylicia. "She was tall and had a long neck, and I guess she looked gawky to herself. But I always thought she was beautiful!"[8]

While admitting she used to think she wasn't pretty, Phylicia believes something different held her back. In her words: "I got most of the jobs I auditioned for. But I have to have a deep purpose. It was only when my work became an avenue to self-recognition, to self-realization, to self-knowledge, that it took on a whole new meaning for me. Otherwise I was content to be good and unheard of. I had the understanding that fame was corrupting. I had seen it happen so many times. But it finally dawned on me that it isn't fame and fortune that's corrupting, it's your understanding of it. And as soon as that happened the slate was wiped clean and the door was open. I was in the chorus of Dreamgirls at that time. I didn't have another job to go to, but I left. I knew I wasn't meant to be an understudy."[9]

Phylicia walked away from *Dreamgirls*, through the open doorway to success, and kept on moving. The talented artist says the practice of meditation helped her to understand her true qualities and make better choices for her life.

Her first big break came when she was chosen to portray a character on a popular daytime drama series, *One Life to Live*.

After a year in that series, there was an opening on *The Cosby Show* for Claire Huxtable, and Phylicia stepped into the role.

The National Association for the Advancement of Colored People (NAACP) honored Phylicia with its "Image Award" for her work on *The Cosby Show*. She was also nominated "Best Supporting Actress in a TV Film" for her role in *Uncle Tom's Cabin*.

In addition to her successful professional life, Phylicia seems to have achieved an ideal family life. She lives in New York with her husband and their daughter, Condola Phylea, and her son, Billy, from a former marriage. Their home is not far from her mother's home and the Adept New American Museum her mother runs. She stays in touch with her mother, to whom she gives credit for greatly influencing her life, and with her brother, who also lives in New York.

Her bond with her sister Debbie is extremely close, even though they live 3,000 miles apart. Debbie lives in Los Angeles with her husband, basketball great Norman Nixon, their daughter, Vivian, and son, Norman, Jr. The sisters phone each other at least once a week. Usually they talk about their families and personal lives, which are much alike.

Professional jealousy has never been a part of the picture. "We had a family motto that if one of us makes it, we all make it," Phylicia said. For us, *making it* wasn't the goal. The goal was achieving excellence and living up to your inherent potential. *Making it* was a side effect — something that happened."[10]

To their credit, when success came along for them, Phylicia and Debbie reached out to others. They finance the museum operated by their mother, and they established a scholarship at Howard University, their alma mater. The $10,000 scholarship, which they founded in memory of their father, is awarded to the most versatile student in the drama department of the university. The student must excel in singing, dancing, and acting.

While it is a privilege to see Phylicia perform as a singer, dancer, or actress, it is an even greater privilege to know the real life Phylicia Rashad, a reserved, elegant, caring person, quietly helping to make room for others to join her at the top.

Ada DeBlanc Simond

Author, Community Leader, Storyteller

Once in a great while a beautiful life lights up the world around it. ADA DeBLANC SIMOND lived that kind of life. Before her death at the age of eighty-five, she had received many tributes and awards that told her how much she was loved for bringing light to others. And she had been inducted into the Texas Women's Hall of Fame as one of the most outstanding citizens of Texas and the United States of America. When she was seventy-eight, still working as a historian, teacher, social and public health worker, writer, wife and mother, she was asked to describe herself. She answered, "I'm just a people person."[1]

When Ada was born in Lake Charles, Louisiana, in November of 1903, her parents, Gilbert and Mathilda DeBlanc, already had three daughters. Girls were not appreciated in those days, so the DeBlancs desperately wanted the new baby to be a boy. When Ada turned out to be a fourth girl they were deeply disappointed. Being the fourth daughter in the family was a serious handicap. Everyone looked down on Ada because she wasn't a boy. And nobody expected her to achieve much in life. In effect, Ada Simond was born socially handicapped into a world that expected little of her. The possibility that Ada might have an outstanding future was never even considered.[2]

Nevertheless, she went on to have many careers in her life. She was an educator, as well as a writer, historian, storyteller, lecturer, newspaper columnist, public health representative, community activist, and court bailiff.

Ada was the child of Creole parents who had no formal education. However, the Catholic church taught the children enough English to read the catechism and prayer book.The DeBlanc family lived in an area where all of the people were much alike even though their homes were miles apart. They lived in a community of Creole mulattos who spoke broken French, and farmed sugar cane, soybeans, rice and other vegetables to support their families. Everyone belonged to the Catholic church. There were no schools in the area, and people sent their children to someone's home for lessons.

The DeBlanc children were sent to the home of Miss Ernest, a spinster who lived nearby. They learned the alphabet from her, and she taught them to read and write. Their first book was the Catholic missal, the church prayer book. Mathilda DeBlanc, their mother, had taught herself to read, and her children learned to read the missal through the help of their mother, the Catholic church, and Miss Ernest.

In those days, there were traveling vendors. A man in a covered wagon would go through the countryside selling items people needed, such as pots and pans, oil for lamps, cloth, needles and thread. He sharpened knives and fixed machines, and he had books. Families used the vendor to trade books with each other. When a family had finished reading a book, the vendor would be asked to drop it off at the house of a neighbor. Other things such as patterns for making clothes were shared the same way.

For Ada, these were pleasant days of sharing wonderful old books from the peddler's wagon with her mother.[3] It was a very special time, when she and her mother were good friends, whispering sweet, girlhood secrets to each other.

When the DeBlanc family moved to Texas, life changed for everyone, including Ada. Three years in a row of extremely bad weather had destroyed her father's crops and caused him to lose the farm. Gilbert DeBlanc had never gone to school. His family taught him to write his name, but except for that, he did not know how to read or write. After he lost his farm, there were bills he could not pay, and he could not find a job.

Then Gilbert and one of his brothers went to Texas looking for work. Gilbert found a job in Austin working for a man who owned a drug store and who catered wedding receptions and anniversary parties. After the family moved to Austin, in addition to caring for her home and children, Mathilda DeBlanc worked as a seamstress. She could design clothes from a picture or a thought.

Now everyone worked, including the children. "There were six of us children," Ada Simond once said, "and we were

Ada DeBlanc Simond

a family of survivors!"[4] Sometimes Mathilda DeBlanc would close the house in Austin and someone would come for the family in a truck or wagon. They would travel to a town miles away to pick cotton. There they would stay in a cabin for a month or as long as it took to pick the field. Describing life after moving to Austin, Ada Simond said:

> We learned to make what we needed from what we had. For example, the stores bought flour, sugar, bran, and chicken feed in thirty-six-inch square muslin bags. We'd buy those bags for twenty-five cents, or the store owner would give them to us, and we'd use them to make clothes, sheets, towels, and curtains. First, we'd soak the bags in cold water to take the writing off, then we'd wash them in ash water that we made by putting ashes in water. After the ashes settled, the water would be like lye, and it would bleach the muslin white and pretty. One bag would make a pillow case, a skirt, a shirt, or a blouse. We sewed four together to make a sheet, and we briar-stitched the seams and embroidered the hems to make it pretty. A bag was cut in half to make a towel or curtain, and in four pieces to make washcloths. We added embroidery, briar-stitching, and crochet for decoration. The things we made were beautiful. Later, merchants began to use cloth with colorful prints for these bags, and instead of writing on the material, they glued on paper labels.

> There wasn't much playing for me as a child. I had lots of responsibilities, but also lots of fun. Whatever we had to do for life was fun. Of course, my brothers played marbles. That was a popular game with boys. And we made up games that helped with our work. I used to make up songs and games that helped to get my little sister to eat or go to bed or bathe. We used lye or old fat from meat drippings, or the crackling dregs left from killing a pig to make our own soap. It wasn't Camay, but it was a good soap that we used for everything, including bathing. We bathed in a big number ten tin tub. We used a smaller foot tub for washing our faces and hands, and feet, which we always washed last. Then we used the sudsy water left from bathing to wash a few clothes or water the garden or scrub the floors. The floors were made of wide pine boards, and we were very protective of them. We powdered every red brick we found, and we used a

baking powder can with holes punched in the top to sprinkle brick powder on the floor. We would brush it in and polish the floor until it was pink and shiny.

On wash days we boiled clothes in a huge, black, iron pot with legs that we set over a fire built in a hole in the ground. Sometimes we used the same fire to cook our food. There might not be a big dinner in the house, but cooking outside while the clothes were boiling made the meal fun.

By the time I was raising children in the 1920s, we had long handled hamburger holders for them to stick in the fire and cook their hamburgers. Sometimes we cooked hot water corn bread or patty cakes in these hamburger holders. You made hot water corn bread by pouring boiling hot water into salted cornmeal. When it was the right consistency, it was baked as corn bread or patted with your hands into a patty cake or rolled into balls to make hush puppies, or it was cooked inside the hamburger holders over a fire.

I miss the love, affection, and companionship that families and communities had in those days. We were all together. If one neighbor was sick, we made soup for the person, washed nightgowns and bedclothes, and went to sit with the sick neighbor for a while.

Ada was eleven years old when the family moved to Austin. There she learned English as a second language. Before she was fourteen, she worked as a housekeeper and as a salesgirl at a concessions stand. She also obtained a job at a business college, where she cleaned classrooms, dictated to stenography students, and corrected spelling and shorthand. In addition, she took courses that were being given at the school.

Ada passed all of her courses and earned a high school diploma. She went on to Tillotson College, was graduated, then attended graduate schools in Iowa, Chicago, and Michigan. She also matriculated at the New York School of Social Work. After she had completed her studies at these institutions, cities from across the nation flooded Ada Simond with offers of lucrative positions. However, she believed strongly that she should return to Austin and give of herself to the city that had given so much to her. Her work in Austin included positions with Tillotson College as a teacher and as a Home Economics Department administrator, and a post as health educator for the Department of Health.

Contributions made by Ada Simond that upgraded society are too numerous to be listed. Many people remember her best as the author of *Mae Dee and Her Family*, a series of historical books about a Black family in Austin. These books preserve for all time the way life was lived by African-Americans in Texas during the early years of Ada's life.[5]

Sponsored by Delta Sigma Theta sorority, these fictionalized stories of Mae Dee and her Austin family are designed to give African-American children in Austin a sense of their own place in the city's history. Much of the information in the stories came from Ada Simond's memories.[6]

In addition to creating literary milestones, Ada Simond distinguished herself by helping to establish important institutions. Austin institutions she helped found include the H. W. Passon Historical Society, Holy Cross Catholic Church, and George Washington Carver Museum.

During her lifetime, she received awards from many organizations, such as the Texas Association for the Study of Afro-American Life and the National Association for the Advancement of Colored People. She was honored by Austin Independent School District, the Texas State Legislature Black Caucus, and the U.S. Congressional Record. In 1974, after she had retired, she began a new career at the request of Judge Herman Jones, a friend for many years. Ada served as bailiff in Judge Jones' Fifty-third District Court for three years.[7] She found the work fascinating and said, "I'm living in another new dimension, witnessing a different kind of human stress . . . another type of human drama."

November 16, 1983, was declared "Ada Simond Day" by the city of Austin.[8] For that day Congress Avenue at Eleventh Street, Austin's main intersection, was renamed "Ada Simond Avenue."

Long before her death, Ada DeBlanc Simond eclipsed the simple goals her mother had wished her to achieve. "My mother wanted me to be a good housekeeper . . . . To cook well, to sew, to crochet, to remember the sick in the neighborhood. All the kinds of things she did," Ada once said. She also said she believed the strong self-reliance and personal confidence that boosted her as an adult came from the trust and confidence her mother placed in her as a little girl. During childhood years, when her mother had depended upon her for polishing floors until they were pretty, looking after her little sister, churning butter, gathering and counting eggs, Ada learned to depend upon herself and gained self-confidence.

As author and storyteller, Ada Simond promoted the importance of being self-sufficient that she learned as a child. Her story of the common spider, for example, praises the insect for being self-reliant, a quality for which she was praised as a girl.[9]

Throughout the public careers and personal life of Ada Simond, one emphasis remained constant: "Everybody is important," she would always say. "Every individual is valuable." And she went to great lengths to make everyone feel special.

As a young woman, Ada married Aubrey Askey. He died when their three children were quite young. Her second marriage to Dr. Charles Yerwood sharpened her awareness of public health needs, and she became a public health representative for the Texas Tuberculosis Association. For twenty-five years she worked educating and informing poor people in Texas about nutrition, hygiene, sanitation, safety, medical services, and other facts about disease prevention. At the age of thirty-seven she became a widow again. Nine years later, she married Luther Simond, distinguished educator in Austin's public school system.

Ada Simond died October 22, 1989, but the rare, loving spirit of Ada DeBlanc Simond lives on in books she wrote, through individuals she nurtured, including this writer, and in the larger society that blossomed from her touch.

"Each of us can succeed at something.
It is for us to discover what that something is, and to make it our goal, remembering that as I travel this road I'm leaving footsteps for another generation, whose safe journey through life I must, to a measure, assure."

Ada M. Simond[10]

Heman Marion Sweatt
Pioneer Fighter for Equal Rights in Education

The year was 1946, and HEMAN MARION SWEATT was at the center of a stormy battle. He wanted to study law at the University of Texas, but he had been denied admission to the all-white school because he was an African-American.

Sweatt knew that many people who disapproved of marriage between persons of different races did not want him admitted to the school. They were afraid that one day he might want to marry one of his white fellow students. Speaking to a mass meeting of people in Austin, Texas, Sweatt introduced his lovely wife, Constantine. "I want to get a legal education at the university, not a wife!" he said.[1] By introducing his wife to the audience, Sweatt was letting everyone know there was nothing to fear because he already had a wife.

A team of lawyers from the National Association for the Advancement of Colored People (NAACP), led by Thurgood Marshall, was representing Sweatt in a suit to force the University of Texas to admit him. Headed by its president, T. S. Painter, the university was resisting every move made by Sweatt and the NAACP.

Sweatt began his struggle to enter the university when he was thirty-three years old. A rather small man, less than five and a half feet tall, already growing bald, he wore glasses and he liked to read. He was a serious, quiet, dignified person, well liked by most people who knew him.

Born in Houston, Texas, December 11, 1912, Heman was the fourth of six children of Ella Rose and James Leonard Sweatt. James Sweatt was a powerful man who set an example for others by acting to solve social problems around him. Employed as a railway mail clerk, shortly before Heman was born James Sweatt helped form a local organization of Black railway mail clerks. The group met once a month to discuss common problems.

When two insurance companies decided not to insure

Heman Marion Sweatt

Black clerks, Heman Sweatt's father and other members of the organization of Black railway mail clerks contacted Black clerks throughout the South. They aimed to establish a way to provide insurance for Black clerks, and to present their grievances to the Post Office Department. By 1913, the Houston organization swelled from thirty-five members into a national organization, the National Alliance of Postal Employees.

Encouraged by his father, Heman attended Wiley College in Marshall, Texas. His major subject was biology. After graduation, he was by turn a porter, grade school teacher, and acting school principal. Later, he entered graduate school at the University of Michigan intending to enroll in medical school. His uncle, Heman Perry, who owned a successful insurance company, helped to supply the necessary money. But when his uncle's business failed, Heman gave up his goal of medical school. Instead, he decided to pursue a public health curriculum at the University of Michigan.

However, the harsh Michigan winter kept Heman feeling ill. After completing two semesters in the cold climate, he returned to Houston for the summer. He found temporary work as a substitute carrier for the post office and decided not to return to the university. In April 1940, he married his high school sweetheart, Constantine Mitchell, and they made their home in Houston.

As a boy, Sweatt had attended NAACP meetings with his father. He had helped raise funds for the organization's lawsuits to achieve racial progress in politics, and worked to register Houston voters. Personally, Sweatt was no stranger to racial prejudice and discrimination. He had been discriminated against because of his race on streetcars, buses, and in public facilities.

At a youth council mass meeting sponsored by the NAACP in 1944, Sweatt gave the main speech. He declared African-Americans would no longer have to bear an inferiority complex put upon them by educators "who spend sleepless nights developing tests aimed at proving mental inferiority of Negro to white . . . instead of . . . opening equal doors of opportunity!"[2]

Following in his father's footsteps, Sweatt had become the local secretary of the National Alliance of Postal Employ-

105

ees. Black Americans working in the post office were subjected to a great deal of discrimination. Postmasters refused to employ African-Americans as clerks, limiting them to lower positions such as postal carriers. And post office regulations required that a person must be employed as a clerk before being appointed to a position as supervisor. Sweatt and his colleagues met with the postmaster and documented their grievances.

In 1944, aided by attorney Francis Scott Key Whittaker, Sweatt prepared legal documents related to the grievances of Black employees that cited national postal regulations and policies. This activity increased Sweatt's interest in the law as a way of challenging discrimination. By the middle of 1945 he decided he wanted to go to law school instead of being a postman.

That fall, Lulu White, the NAACP's state director of branches, spoke to a group of Aframericans at Wesley Chapel. She asked for a volunteer to file a lawsuit against the university of Texas. When it seemed no one else was going to respond, Heman Sweatt stood up. He said he was willing to attempt to enroll in the law school of the University of Texas with the support of the NAACP.

Wholeheartedly behind his son, James Sweatt announced Heman's decision at a large family dinner one Sunday. There were a few doubts. One person thought Heman, at thirty-three, was too old to begin a law career. Another said the Sweatt family did not have enough money to fight the state of Texas over racism in America.

Constantine was not eager for her husband to volunteer to be a guinea pig. She was afraid he might lose his job, and their house. She feared they would be targets of racial violence. But when the discussion was over, the family fully supported Heman.

On February 26, 1946, Heman Sweatt arrived at the University of Texas at Austin with a delegation from the NAACP. They were met at the registrar's office by university officials, including President T. S. Painter. Sweatt offered his transcript and asked to be admitted to the university's law school.

Bragging that he had no more "than the normal amount

of prejudice against Negroes," the registrar, E. J. Matthews, tried to change Sweatt's mind. He said the university would make funds available for Black students to be educated somewhere else. He warned that Blacks would lose everything if a lawsuit were filed. Sweatt declined the university's offer, and President Painter accepted his application, saying he would hold it until he received a ruling from the attorney general.

Painter informed the attorney general that Sweatt was qualified "except for the fact that he is a Negro." On March 16, Attorney General Grover Sellers ruled to uphold "Texas' wise and long-continued policy of segregation." Painter mailed the ruling with a letter of rejection to Sweatt.[3] On May 16, Sweatt filed suit against Painter and other university officials seeking to compel the University of Texas to admit him to its school of law.

The court proceedings crept along through hearings, petitions, appeals, trial courts, and decisions that called for new trials. Meanwhile, a number of new ideas and special plans for educating African-American law students were being tried. The University of Texas offered to provide funds for Aframerican students to be educated at a school in another state. The state legislature introduced a bill that authorized the African-American college at Prairie View, Texas, to teach law or any other subject taught at the University of Texas. Further, to make all things seem equal, the legislators changed the name of the college to *Prairie View University.*

At one point, an arrangement was made for two African-American attorneys to teach a law course in their offices. Finally, a makeshift "law school" for African-American students was opened in the basement of a building leased from a petroleum company.

These plans failed to attract a single student. Far from it! They convinced Thurgood Marshall that African-American students could not receive a suitable education segregated from others. In an earlier case, Marshall had led the team of NAACP lawyers in a suit demanding that African-Americans be provided with equal opportunities for achieving an education. Now the team changed its goal.

The new approach sought to prove that separating African-Americans from others was a way of discriminating against them. Also, that this policy did not provide "equal protection" which the Fourteenth Amendment to the U.S. Constitution guaranteed American citizens.

The more Heman Sweatt saw of the NAACP lawyers in action, the more he wanted to become a lawyer. Marshall directed the case and wrote most of the brief with the help of others on the NAACP legal staff. James Nabrit, Jr., from the faculty of Howard University's law school, was a powerful courtroom attorney. In examining witnesses, Nabrit showed that the basement law school was inferior to the law school of the University of Texas.

Nabrit relentlessly cross-examined Charles McCormick, dean of both law schools, drawing from his personal knowledge of the requirements for a legal education. McCormick was forced to admit the basement school was opened only part-time, had an inadequate library, and offered no extracurricular activities. Also, he admitted that the basement school was not accredited and lacked prestige.

By the time McCormick left the witness stand, the state's case was practically destroyed. Nabrit's interrogation had been so devastating that Marshall would not let him question Helen Hargrave, a white woman. Fearing that Nabrit's bruising style of questioning aimed at a white woman would cause an unfavorable reaction from the press, Marshall questioned Helen Hargrave himself.

As the litigation wore on and on, the strain of being the plaintiff in the case weighed heavily on Heman Sweatt. At work, he was the victim of constant pressures including threats on his life. At home, his wife was continually harassed by vicious phone calls and letters. The Sweatt house was defaced with paint, its windows smashed.

Eventually the case reached the United States Supreme Court. On June 5, 1950, the highest court in the country announced its decision while Heman Sweatt was delivering mail in Houston. His wife was first to tell him the news. Then he listened to radio reports. The telephone rang, and the voice of Thurgood Marshall came through the phone congratulating Sweatt. "We won the big one!" Marshall exclaimed.[4]

The Supreme Court had reached a unanimous decision which was announced by Chief Justice Fred Vinson. The Court concluded that African-American law students had not been offered educational opportunities equal to those available at the University of Texas. The opinion included many examples of the inferiority of the educational opportunities which the university had made available for African-American students.

On September 19, 1950, while reporters watched and asked questions, and the cameras of photographers flashed, Sweatt registered at the University of Texas. He was now thirty-seven, four and a half years older than when he first attempted to apply. He had been weakened physically and emotionally from his ordeal as plaintiff. At the beginning of the lawsuit, he had said he felt he "could lick the world!" Now, he described himself as a "complete emotional wreck."[5]

From his first day on the university's Austin campus, he was given a mixed reception. Some professors were friendly and encouraging. Others insulted him. The new dean rebuked Sweatt for the publicity he received at registration, and warned him against any "NAACP showmanship."[6]

Most fellow students were pleasant toward Sweatt and other Black students. They had few problems at lounges, eating places, drinking fountains, and sports events. In fact, Sweatt was appointed to serve on the class social committee.

On the other hand, ugly incidents were plentiful. For example, after studying late in the library the first Friday night of the semester, Sweatt walked toward his car. Across the street, a large crowd with a huge burning cross was waiting for him. In the company of a white friend, Sweatt reached the car unharmed. Then they discovered the tires on his car had been slashed.

Such incidents made Sweatt understand that many people wanted him to fail. At the same time, from within himself and from others around him, he felt pressure to excel. It was hard to concentrate on his studies.

Although he found the work interesting and devoted a great deal of time to study, he did not excel. After receiving failing grades the first year, he returned in the fall to audit the courses he had not passed.

In the spring, he again enrolled as a regular student. But that was his last semester at the University of Texas. During his time at the school, he suffered poor health that included ulcers and an appendicitis operation which forced him to miss classes for seven weeks.

Sweatt was deeply disappointed at his failure. He had worked hard and been hampered by health problems and financial difficulties, yet he blamed himself. So many burdens placed a constant strain on his relationship with his wife. In the end, Constantine returned to Houston and the couple was divorced.

In the summer of 1952, Sweatt also returned to Houston, his hopes of becoming a lawyer crushed, his personal life shattered. He received a scholarship to study at the Graduate School of Social Work at Atlanta University. There he earned a master's degree in 1954. He then moved to Cleveland, Ohio, and worked for the NAACP and the National Urban League. Later, he returned to Atlanta, remarried, and continued to work with organizations dedicated to social progress.

Heman Marion Sweatt played a vital part in the struggle of Black Americans for civil rights. Because he stood fast in his battle for the right to attend the University of Texas, racially segregated colleges and universities across the nation admitted African-Americans. Sweatt's courage and determination provided strength for the *Brown v. Board of Education* victory. In 1954, that landmark case overturned legal racial segregation in all U.S. public education.

Florence Wolfe ("Lady Flo")
Cattle Rancher

FLORENCE WOLFE was born in Illinois in the late 1860s. Although she was an African-American woman who lived at a time when few women or Aframericans were well educated, she was a high school graduate. This was an outstanding achievement for that time. She told friends she attended high school in Ohio. She also said she attended school with the famous lawyer and politician William Jennings Bryan.

Life changed for Flo when she met an African-American colonel. Young, adventurous, and in love with the thought of a wonderful life with the colonel, she ran away with him. He took her to El Paso, Texas. But her dream of an exciting, romantic life with the colonel was not to be. He abandoned her.

Flo took a position as housekeeper for the family of a wealthy rancher. As she worked, she studied the life around her and quietly taught herself the ranching business. She learned what a rancher needed to know about cattle, how to manage them, how to run the ranch, how to regulate and control ranch hands. After three years, the family sold the ranch. Once again, Flo's life changed dramatically.

She moved to El Paso and got a job as a barmaid. Among the men who frequented the bar was an English nobleman. Nobody knew his exact title, but people called him Lord Beresford. He had come to Texas in 1889 and bought Los Ojitos, a 250,000-acre ranch.

Beresford was highly educated, but he didn't know anything about ranching. People said he didn't have the "horse sense" needed to operate a ranch. They also said his formal education could not take the place of ranching experience.

Everyone knew that the Englishman was a remittance man. This meant that he lived on a remittance, a sum of money sent to him ever so often by his family in England. He lived in a large, sprawling, adobe house. His neighbors said the house was built in 1760. It was also believed that Apaches had plundered and abandoned the house.

Beresford employed a number of American and Spanish-American cowboys to run the ranch for him. Most of his hired hands were outlaws, and most of them were dishonest. To add to this unfortunate mix, Lord Beresford was a drunkard. So it is easy to understand that although the Englishman received large sums of money from his relatives in England, he was going broke.

About this time he received a stroke of good luck which

seemed to be a terrible blow when it happened. On one of his drinking trips to El Paso, Beresford fell deathly ill with pneumonia.

It was his habit to visit the bars in El Paso with two of his English friends who owned an adjoining ranch. But when he got sick, his friends went "bar hopping" without him. When the two Englishmen came to the bar where Flo worked, and their friend was not with them, Flo was curious. "Where is Lord Beresford tonight?" she asked.

"He's sick, Flo," she was told. "Beresford is at the hotel., and he's going to die."

Without another word, Flo removed her apron and headed for the hotel. She told the owner she wanted to be a nurse to Lord Beresford. The hotel owner gave her permission to stay and nurse the English nobleman.

Lord Beresford went through a long, difficult illness. Through it all, Flo was there. Slowly, she nursed him back to health. When he was finally able to go home, he took her with him.

Soon after Flo arrived on the ranch, things changed. For the first time, the ranch was managed properly. Cowhands got up in the morning, went out on the grounds and performed their chores as never before.

Clearly, Flo knew what needed to be done, and how to get it done. The cowboys complained bitterly, of course, but for the first time since Beresford bought the place, they really worked. And Los Ojitos began to thrive.

Ordinarily, meals were eaten in the dining room of the bunkhouse where the ranch hands lived. But when neighboring ranchers or members of their families visited the Beresford home, Flo always set the table in the big house.

Once Mrs. Boyd, who lived on a neighboring ranch, was traveling with her daughter, and the two stopped for the night at the Los Ojitos big house. When Flo announced that dinner was served, she showed the women to a table beautifully set for two.

"Flo, you're my hostess. It embarrasses me to accept your hospitality and not have you dine with me," Mrs. Boyd said.

"Mrs. Boyd, I know how Southern women feel about Negroes," Flo replied. "It would be very embarrassing to me to eat with you."

Then, while the two women ate, Flo remained standing, talking with them about her past.

Memories of the Boyd family are largely responsible for preserving the history of Lady Flo and Lord Beresford. For example, the Boyds learned that Los Ojitos cowboys were branding half the cattle on Beresford's ranch for Lord Beresford, and half for Flo, or Lady Flo as she was now called. This information was discovered when cowboys from the two ranches worked together during round-ups.

Rancher Boyd chuckled when he learned about the double branding going on at Los Ojitos. He laughed harder when he found out that Lord Beresford did not understand that cattle with Flo's brand legally belonged to her. Boyd spoke to Flo and she admitted that she had recorded her brand, and that Beresford did not realize the meaning of what she had done.

"You are doing a lot for this ranch," Boyd told her.

"I want to run this place so that it is self-supporting," she answered. "Then the money that comes from England can be used to buy more land."

While Beresford was selling his cattle, Flo let hers accumulate. However, she studied the market and advised him when to sell, and what price he should get for his stock. When the decision was made to put a fence around the massive range, Flo supervised the work and managed the financing for the enormous job.

Within three years, Beresford bought another gigantic land tract. But despite his business progress, he continued his drinking bouts. One day, one of rancher Boyd's sons visited Los Ojitos shortly after noon and found Beresford "very drunk."

According to him, Flo was at the head of the table, and was also drinking, but only a little. With cowboys, horse-buyers and young Boyd at the table, Beresford and Flo began quarreling. Finally they began throwing biscuits at each other. When they ran out of biscuits, Lady Flo hurled a plate at him.

"Lady Flo," young Boyd pleaded, "please don't throw any more! You might hit me!"

113

The Battle of the Biscuits ended with everybody laughing.

In time, Beresford hired this same son of Boyd as foreman for Los Ojitos. "I had frequent consultations with Flo," he recalls, ". . . I realized how very shrewd she was, and how honest."

Los Ojitos and the new ranch were doing so well that Beresford decided to expand even more. He boarded a train for Minnesota, where he planned to select pastures for his cattle. Many cattle ranchers in the Southwest drove their cattle to Montana, the Dakotas, or Minnesota to fatten them on good grass in those states.

As the train chugged along, Beresford was relaxing in the smoking car. Suddenly, the train lurched and spun off the tracks. Cars were overturned, baggage and personal possessions of travelers were flung wide. Passengers in most of the train's coaches were unharmed. A few people in the smoking car were injured. But, Lord Beresford was killed.

His older brother, Sir Charles, came from England to claim the money and property that had belonged to Lord Beresford. He hired an El Paso attorney to take the legal steps required to process the inheritance.

When the attorney asked what, if anything, he planned to allow Flo to keep, Sir Charles was stunned. He had never heard of Flo! Asked if Lord Beresford ever mentioned any friends, Sir Charles recalled the name of Mr. Boyd and went to see him.

"This Negress," he said "seems to feel that she is entitled to a share of my brother's property. Both the attorney in El Paso and my brother's banker advised me to see you."

Boyd responded thoughtfully. "When she took over Los Ojitos your brother was close to bankruptcy," he said. "He was drinking so much that he was incapable of handling the ranch. Flo put it on a business basis. She paid the debts, helped him accumulate land, and guided his investments. In consequence, the property, not including cattle, is worth $250,000.

"Half or more of them [the cattle] are in her brand. Those, nobody can touch. The rest are worth, at market price, easily $50,000."

"But she wants a share of the land! How much can she get?" the brother asked.

"Not being an attorney, I couldn't say. But if you can get her to settle out of court for $100,000, you are fortunate."

"A hundred thousand dollars! That's a big sum!"

"Without Flo, your brother would have left no estate. And if this case comes to trial, I'll be the principal witness. If you don't subpoena me, Flo will. Your brother was my friend, but if I'm put under oath to tell the truth, that's just what I'll do. Again, I'm going to suggest that you attempt to arrange a fair settlement and avoid publicity that would cause embarrassment to you and your family."

Some say that Sir Charles took Boyd's advice and settled with Lady Flo for $100,000. Others insist she only received about $10,000, which she skillfully used to build greater wealth.

Lady Flo had never been a drunkard, as Lord Beresford had been, but after he died, she gave up strong drink. A beautiful, bright woman who spoke Spanish fluently, she now considered herself Lord Beresford's widow. She bought a home in El Paso and placed a concrete block with the words "LADY FLO" in front of the house. She also required her neighbors and friends to call her Lady Flo.

Her business skills were put to use in a second property which she purchased as an investment. Situated on the lot next to her home, the building had four units which she rented out. In addition, she used the property to conduct social programs designed to uplift her people.

Lady Flo was friendly with her neighbors, who respected her for being well educated and showing concern for the poor. She would often buy food left from church suppers and give it to needy people.

The beautiful cattle rancher died of tuberculosis in 1913. Her death certificate stated that she was forty-seven. She was buried in Concordia Cemetery in a simple grave that now is hard to find. But the legend of how she turned a ne'er-do-well English lord into a rich, respectable businessman, and used her own wealth to help others, will live on forever.

Marian E. Barnes
Counselor, Writer, Storyteller,
Author of this book

The first exciting event in my life happened in the Atlantic Ocean. When I was a baby, my dad swam far into the ocean holding me over his head. On the shore, my mother waited, afraid and anxious, wanting him to swim back and place me safely in her arms.

Sometimes, I think I remember feeling waves splash me a little, and tasting a bit of salty ocean water on my tongue as he swam. But that is my imagination making pictures of the story I have heard so often. I really do not remember being in the ocean.

The first thing I truly remember is looking at miles and miles of bright blue sky and pretty, white clouds, while hearing Johnny Ace sing me a lullaby. Johnny lived next door to me in North Philadelphia. He was a little boy, and I was about a year old. Every day he asked my mother if he could "hold the baby." As he sat on the front steps cradling me in his arms, I saw the big, blue sky and fleecy clouds above, and I heard him singing a lullaby: *Tiny baby brother, Play that I am mother . . .*

Years later, a singer named Johnny Ace became famous. Whenever I heard his voice on the radio, I saw blue sky and clouds. I wanted to ask him if he was my friend who had sung me to sleep so many times. I wanted him to sing the rest of the song and tell me the words I could not remember. But Johnny Ace died before I could speak to him. Nevertheless, I believe he was the singing little boy who was my first friend.

My next memory is of being in a hospital when I was three. I was very ill and had to have lung surgery, but I was angry because I was in a hospital. So when members of my family came to see me, I would not speak to them. One day my mother and another relative visited the hospital. They tried to talk to me for a long time, but I would not utter a word.

Finally, they stood up to leave. I felt so sad I thought my

heart would break. I tried hard not to cry. I didn't want them to know I cared that they were leaving. But as they walked away, sadness overwhelmed me, and I burst into tears!

When at last my family came to take me home, I clung to a nurse and said I wanted to stay where I was! I think that was my way of getting even with my relatives for leaving me in the hospital. However, for the rest of my life, now and then someone would say, "You can't pay any attention to the way Marian acts. Remember what she did in the hospital!"

I was born in Ridgeland, South Carolina, in 1923. Shortly after my birth, my family moved to Philadelphia. The ways that people earned a living were changing. Farms and plantations that had supported life in the South were closing. As a result, so many African-Americans moved north that the event is sometimes called "The Great Migration."

Some Black families left the South to seek jobs. Others left to escape violence, Jim Crow laws, hate and disrespect against African-Americans that were at their worst in the South. My father was one of these people. He had educated himself to earn a living as a carpenter, salesman or farmer. But one day, in a lumber shop, a group of Caucasian men were talking about African-American women. They said disrespectful things in loud voices so my father could hear them.

If my dad had answered these men, he might have been killed, leaving no one to provide for his wife and six children. But having to remain silent ripped my father's soul. Although he never repeated what the men said, he was tormented by the memory of their conversation in the lumber store for the rest of his life. "I decided to leave the South standing in that store," he would say. "I said to myself, 'There has to be a better place than this!'" And though many years had passed, you could always hear the pain he was still feeling in his voice.

At twelve, I tried to teach myself to swim. My mother and aunt were on a bench beside the swimming pool doing needlework. Tired of trying to swim, I started stepping slowly toward deep water. Each step brought the water higher. It reached my chest and I knew I should turn back. *One more step will bring the water up to my chin. Then I'll turn back,* I thought. I took one more step, my foot hit a slide, and I slipped into deep water and began bobbing up and down. I tried to shout for help, but my mouth filled with water and I went down to the bottom of the pool and came up again.

I grabbed my nose and held it to keep from drowning. A girl who was an excellent swimmer sat on the rope that divided deep and shallow water. She stared at me, but she made no move to help. With my eyes I begged her to help me, or call someone. But her eyes were cold as ice. Silently, I pleaded with her. But she did not budge.

Lips pressed tight, her icy eyes fixed on mine, she sat so still she might have been carved in stone. Many, many children were playing in the pool. How could a lifeguard see one small girl quietly bobbing up and down, quietly about to die?

Still looking up to the strange, unresponsive girl and holding my nose, I gave up hope that help would come. Then without warning, the body of the lifeguard knifed through the air, split the water, and his strong arms pulled me to safety. The unfriendly girl on the rope had helped me in spite of herself. Obviously, the lifeguard saw her sitting on the rope staring into the water and, following her eyes, saw I was about to drown.

I ran to my mother and aunt, who sat chatting and sewing as though nothing had happened. "Didn't you see me? I almost drowned," I said to my mother.

"I know," she said calmly. "Did you thank the lifeguard for saving your life?" In the excitement, I had not thought of thanking him. "I think you should find him now and thank him," she said. "He was not a young man. Pulling you out of the water seemed to be very hard for him."

I found the lifeguard. "Thank you for saving my life," I said. His pale, white, sun-reddened skin flushed even redder with embarrassment as I thanked him. But I knew he appreciated my thanks.

I learned to love words from my parents. Their language was colorful and fun as they talked about everyday things. My mother was a Mrs. Malaprop with some people's names. She did not address these people by name, perhaps to avoid making an embarrassing mistake. But she spoke of her friend Mrs. Money as "Mrs. Penny" and of Mrs. Hammer as "Mrs.

Hatchet." One member of our church often prayed out loud for a husband at prayer meetings. Her name was Sister Desfores, but Mother referred to her as "Sister Desperate"! If someone was in the intensive care unit of a hospital, my mother said the person was in "expensive care."

Whenever my parents were upset or angry, they used words that sent me to a dictionary. For instance, when my father sternly told someone to "countermand" an order. Or when my mother, annoyed with some friends, accused them of having held their "caucus."

I learned words from my mother, but I was never able to think of the right word to use as swiftly as she could. For instance, in high school, I was offered a job through the National Youth Administration, or NYA. The counselor arranged jobs for white students in offices, laboratories, and institutions. However, she offered me a job as a maid in a private home. I refused that job only to be offered a similar one which I also did not accept. After I had turned down numerous maid jobs, the counselor said, "Marian, I think you do not want to take a job as a maid. There is nothing degrading about doing housework!"

"I know," I answered. "But I don't want that kind of job."

I couldn't get home fast enough to tell my mother what had happened. "What should I have told her when she said there was nothing degrading about housework?" I asked.

"You should have said, 'There is nothing elevating about it either!'" my mother snapped.

The words I learned at home helped me to enjoy books. Reading taught me many things and took me into a hundred worlds. At home in the evenings I read by the light of an oil lamp. One night when I was very young, the light from the lamp was so dim it was hard to see the words on the book. Trying to see better, I kept leaning closer and closer to the lamp on the table. All at once, I heard a sizzling sound and felt a sharp pain. Until this day there is a round burn mark on the skin of my forehead left from the night it "kissed" a kerosene lamp!

When I was ten, my parents took me to visit the South. I was elated! The trip taught me a lot about racial prejudice. Often there were no restaurants or restrooms to serve African-Americans. Sometimes we had to use special doors or areas or water fountains marked *"COLORED."* Some roadside food stands had price signs with different prices on each side. When African-American customers drove up, these merchants turned the price signs around to show a higher price.

Driving along the highway, we saw huge "KKK" letters carved into the barks of the trees. In Lynchburg, Virginia, one or two *"K"*s were carved on trees too small for three letters. My father told me that when he was young such towns posted signs that said: *"Nigger read and run. If you can't read, run anyhow."*

As we traveled, I was surprised to see poor, down-trodden, unkempt white people who looked listless, unwashed, and underfed. I had lived in African-American neighborhoods where the store owners were white, and better off than most Black Americans. I did not realize that white people could be poor, untidy, and hungry.

One day, in Ridgeland, South Carolina, a little girl with pale, milky skin, golden curls, and blue eyes came to her front gate as I was walking by. She was clutching a doll that looked exactly like her. Her eyes fastened on mine, her lip curled, and she said, almost singing, "You nigger, you! You nigger, you!" I looked at her for a moment and I thought, *I have got to sock this little girl — HARD.*

I grabbed her dress near her throat and held it tightly so that she would be a firm, sure target and the punch would hurt more. The girl stretched her eyes and mouth in disbelief and fear. I drew my fist back to hit her. Just before I brought it down, something told me to draw my hand back further so the blow would be harder. I raised my fist back further, and higher, then higher again. The little girl's blue eyes kept getting wider and wider, keeping time with my fist rising in the air. I was about to smash it into her face, when that something talked again and said, "Take your fist back even further, so it will hurt even more."

Again I listened to that voice, and it was my undoing. I took my fist as far back and as high as it could go. This was it! I was going to slam it into that nasty, scared face and mouth and get the greatest feeling in the world! Just as my mighty

120

fist reached its apex and I was satisfied it would do the best job possible, my father and mother, who were walking in front of me, turned around. *"MARIAN!"* My mother's terrified scream filled the street, freezing my fist in midair.

Now I was sorry I had wasted time drawing my fist back. I kept thinking that if I hadn't been so intent on hitting her as hard as possible, I would at least have hit her. As it was, except for the stupid, scared look on her ugly face, she had gotten away with what she had said.

Those were my thoughts that day and for a long time afterward. But when I grew up and understood what the South was like then, my ideas changed. I realized if I had struck the other child, it could have brought violence, even destruction, to my parents and me.

There were good times in South Carolina: running with the children from a rain shower moving across the land toward us; gathering warm eggs from the hen house; drinking fresh cow's milk. The milk was bitter, and grown-ups said that was because the cow had eaten grass just before she was milked. I wanted to learn to milk the cow. But when I tried to pull the cow teat, it felt soft and mushy. Unpleasantly surprised, I jumped away and fell into a pile of cow manure!

One day my parents showed me the house where I was born, a beautiful two-story cottage my father had built. It was the first two-story house ever built in Ridgeland. White trimmed in red, set among grass and trees, it was prettier than houses in Philadelphia where we lived. I was awed by my father's handiwork on that house.

I also saw a house built by another relative. From front porch to roof, it was made of soft drink cans instead of bricks. Sometimes this house was rented to white people, either tourists or schoolteachers on vacation. But it was empty when we saw it. The teachers had told the owner if he ever rented the house to people of his own race, they would never rent it from him again.

On another day, while Mother shopped in a store, I skipped about outside picking flowers. What fun! I felt like a child in stories I had read. When Mother saw what I had done, she explained that the flowers had been planted by the storekeeper, and they belonged to her. Then Mother took me inside the shop to apologize.

The store owner's eyes were sad as she looked at her dead flowers. I had picked every blossom in her garden! The flowers had wilted as soon as I gripped them in my sweaty hands. But she was gracious, and showed no hate or disrespect because we were not of the same race as she was.

While we were in the South, I met my dad's father. A quiet man, he spoke to me only once. As I sat beside him on the porch of his home, he suddenly struck my thigh and said, "Pull your dress down, daughter!"

I now know he was trying to teach me that I was growing up and it was time for me to "sit like a lady" as girls were taught at that time. Nowadays most adults know it is important to explain things they say to a child. But in those days, grown-ups usually did not talk with children. "Children should be seen and not heard," they said. Or, "Speak when you are spoken to, and come when you are called." Today most people realize such statements can harm a child in ways that last for life.

When I was about eight, I became a storyteller. By then, my dad was a minister, and a wonderful storyteller. Also, because of the Great Depression, few people had money for theaters or concerts. So folks entertained themselves by giving programs which included music and storytelling.

In elementary school, I told my classmates stories I had heard or read. When students were restless, the teacher would say, "Marian, tell a story." By the time I was in junior high school, I was writing poetry and prose. Once a teacher did not believe I had written the prose homework assignment he received from me. "If you could write like that you would be paid for it," he said.

Much later, I studied writing at Temple University in Philadelphia. Then I became a writer and reporter for radio and TV for a time. Afterward, I attended Villanova University and earned a graduate degree in counseling and human relations.

In my early twenties, I wrote a novel, *The Roaring Bottom*. Nearly fifty years passed before it was published.[1] But I am glad I did not lose faith in the manuscript and throw it away. Readers have said they enjoyed the book, or learned from it. And I am happy that in the future readers can continue to enjoy and study the story.

I hope my experience will encourage young readers to hold on to their dreams no matter what happens to make them seem impossible. And to understand that if they believe in themselves, they can achieve whatever they desire no matter who does not believe in them. Ever so often, I am asked to speak to young people about life values. It is a tremendous challenge.

How do I tell young people to feel great respect for themselves, and to treat themselves with great respect? To learn and grow by reading everything possible? To reach out, touch and learn from people around them, and things around them? To claim the brightest star as their own and keep climbing until it is theirs? This is what I say:

*Your spirit is the most important part of you. **Nurture** it continuously. Each of you can do something that nobody else can do to make the world a better place. Study yourself as a person. Learn who you are and what you can do. Study the history of your people. Read. Read. Read. Reach. Reach. Reach. Then **LEAP** for the stars!*

Notes / Glossary

Debbie Allen

  1. *"SISTERS:* Debbie Allen and Phylicia Rashad," *McCall's* magazine, July 1987.
  2. *Current Biography Yearbook,* 1987.
  3. *"SISTERS:* Debbie Allen and Phylicia Rashad," *McCall's* magazine, July 1987.
  4. *Ibid.*
  5. *Current Biography Yearbook,* 1987.
  6. *"SISTERS:* Debbie Allen and Phylicia Rashad," *McCall's* magazine, July 1987.
  7. *Ibid.*
  8. *Ibid.*
  9. *Ibid.*
  10. *Ibid.*
  11. *Current Biography Yearbook,* 1987.
  12. *"SISTERS:* Debbie Allen and Phylicia Rashad," *McCall's* magazine, July 1987.
  13. *Ibid.*
  14. *Ibid.*
  15. *Current Biography Yearbook,* 1987.

choreographer: dance composer and arranger.
deceased: no longer living; dead.
director: supervisor of acting, lighting, music, and rehearsals for a show.
discipline: the training of the mind and character; a way of life in accordance with rules.
fickle: not steadfast; changeable.
harks: listens closely.
passionate: easily moved to strong emotion; intense.
producer: one who brings a play or movie before the public, arranges financial backing, etc.
Sweet Charity: Famous Broadway hit production which enjoyed a record-breaking run, for which Debbie Allen received her second Tony nomination (1986–1987).
trauma: a physical wound or injury; a violent emotional blow.
versatility: the quality of doing many different kinds of things well.

Vivian Ayers

1. Ruthe Winegarten, *Black Texas Women: 150 Years of Trial and Triumph* (Austin: University of Texas Press, 1995).
2. *"SISTERS:* Debbie Allen and Phylicia Rashad," *McCall's* magazine, July 1987.
3. *Jet* magazine, November 7, 1988.
4. *Ibid.*
5. *Ibid.*
6. *Women's News,* Volume 13, Number 6, February 1995, Westchester/Rockland. (Harrison, NY), Alan Petrucelli.
7. *Ibid.*
8. *Ibid.*

allure: attraction; charm.
ancients: persons who lived many years ago.
cascade: a waterfall; to fall as or like a waterfall.
choreographer: a dance arranger.
cosmetologist: beautician.
culture: customary beliefs; social forms and material traits of a racial, religious or social group.
curator: a person in charge of a museum.
destiny: a course of events determined in advance.
essential: necessary.
Mayan: pertaining to original American peoples chiefly of Central America.
myriad: very many.
offspring: a child or children.
phenomenal: extraordinary, unusual.
spacious: large or magnificent in scale.

John Biggers

1. Alwyn Barr and Robert A. Calvert, *Black Leaders: Texans for Their Times* (Austin: Texas State Historical Association, 1981).
2. *Ibid.*
3. *Ibid.*
4. *Ibid.*
5. *Ibid.*
6. *Ibid.*
7. *Ibid.*
8. *Ibid.*
9. *Ibid.*
10. *Ibid.*
11. *Ibid.*
12. *Ibid.*
13. *Ibid.*
14. *Ibid.*

aesthetics: ideas and understanding of the nature of art or beauty.

African-Americans: Black Americans who descended from original Africans.

amputated: cut off, especially by surgery.

Caucasians: members of the race of people who usually have approximately white skin, and generally descend from Europeans.

creative: having the ability to make or produce something using imagination or skill.

creativity: the ability to make something.

defiled: made unclean or impure.

demeaned: lowered in standard or dignity; degraded.

draftsman: a person who makes plans, drawings, or draws up documents; an artist who excels at drawing.

emancipation: the act or process of being set free, especially from slavery after the Civil War.

emeritus: an honorary title given after retirement which corresponds to the position last held during active service.

functional: useful.

gangrene: death of soft tissues caused when blood stops coming to a part of the body.

impulses: sudden desires to do something.

influence: to sway; to indirectly affect or change.

interrelationship: connected or shared purpose or activity.

ordinance: an order made by a ruling body.

paternalistic: of or relating to a father.

perception: understanding.

reflected: shown as an image.

revolutionize: to overthrow; to change completely.

rural: out in the country.

tuition: the price charged for instruction.

Mary Branch

1. Jenness, *Twelve Negro Americans,* 89.
2. Alwyn Barr, and Robert A. Calvert, *Black Leaders: Texans for Their Times* (Austin: Texas State Historical Association, 1981).

aloof: away, cold in manner; at a physical or spiritual distance.

alma mater: a school which one has attended.

boycott: to join others in refusing to have any dealings with an individual, group, or business.

coeducational: providing for the education of both sexes in one institution.

corruption: moral decay; dishonesty.

domestic: related to the home or house.

edifices: buildings; beautiful buildings.

integrity: moral soundness; honesty.

merit: excellence, deserving praise.
nepotism: favoritism shown by hiring relatives.
pedagogy: the science or profession of teaching.
scraggly: rough and uneven.

Bessie Coleman

adrift: afloat without control; loose.
aerodynamics: the science of air flow.
Aframerican: Black American descendant of original Africans; an African-American.
African-American: Black American descendant of original Africans; an Aframerican.
ascending: rising, mounting.
aviatrix: a woman airplane pilot.
brilliant: very bright; glittering.
Caucasian: of or relating to the white race of human beings.
colleague: a fellow worker.
commemorated: recalled to memory.
discrimination: differentiation; the making of a difference in the way certain people or races are treated or served.
ejected: thrown out; forced out.
enslaved: one who has been made the property of another; someone forced to become a slave.
exclaiming: crying out with emotion or excitement.
hurtling: moving (something) with great force and noise.
inferior: situated below another.
intelligent: smart; quick-thinking; capable of thinking, reasoning, and using knowledge to solve problems well.
Jim Crow: laws and traditions that discriminate against Africans and Aframericans.
lynched: killed by a mob.
malfunctioned: failed to operate properly.
meteor: a solid body from outer space which glows as it enters earth's atmosphere.
prejudice: to hold thoughts and/or feelings that cause a fixed opinion (usually unfavorable) about certain people, groups, or situations.
proclaiming: announcing publicly or officially.
rebuffed: impolitely rejected.
sabotaged: deliberate damage done to property.
segregated: separated.

Wilhelmina Ruth Fitzgerald Delco

1. Alberta Brooks, *Our Texas,* Winter 1995. Edited by General Berry, Jr.

African-Americans: Black American descendants of original Africans; Aframericans.

alma mater: one's school or university.

bailiff: a court officer who keeps order in court.

commitment: mental or emotional drive linked to strong belief or action.

Communists: members of the Communist Party or movement who believe property should not be owned by individuals but should belong to all in common.

dedication: self-sacrificing devotion.

emeritus: one retired from professional life but permitted to hold the rank of his/her last office as an honorary title.

extracurricular: organized activities connected with school but carrying no academic credit.

integrity: moral soundness.

landmarks: events that mark a turning point or a stage.

lapel: the part of the front of a dress or coat folded back near the neckline.

legislature: a law-making body, often composed of a House of Representatives and a Senate.

patron saint: a saintly, spiritual guardian to a person, group, place, etc.

probation officer: an officer appointed to investigate, report on, and supervise conduct of convicted offenders on probation.

protégé: someone guided by another, especially being helped in a career.

Three Divas on Stage

1. Ruthe Winegarten, *Black Texas Women — 150 Years of Trial and Triumph.* (Austin: University of Texas Press, 1995).

2. LBJ: Lyndon Baines Johnson, former president of the United States.

3. Margaret Perry, director of education for Austin Lyric Opera; Geneva Rawlins, director of music, Wesley United Methodist Church.

a cappella: not accompanied by musical instruments.

alumnae: female former students of a school.

aura: the air that surrounds something or someone.

divas: chief women singers in an opera or concert.

rafters: sloping beams that form a roof framework.

vitality: the quality of being alive.

Dr. Virgie Maye Carrington DeWitty

anthems: songs of praise or joy, often having many parts and sung by groups with many voices.

atmosphere: the gases that surround the earth.

diva: the title given a female opera or concert singer; usually the most respected singer among the best singers of her kind.

estate: property and debts left after a person's death.

eternal: lasting forever.

gospel songs: African-American spiritual songs.

Houston Astrodome: a "bubble-top" stadium that seats 65,000 people in Houston, Texas.

hymns: songs of praise, worship, prayer, or request, usually more simple than anthems.

mentor: an experienced and trusted advisor.

pervade: to spread throughout and into every part of.

Dr. Beulah Agnes Curry Jones

coached: trained intensively by instruction.

curler bonnet: a cover placed on the head to hide curlers.

dedication: self-sacrificing devotion; faithfulness.

diligently: industriously; tirelessly.

expertise: expert knowledge.

formal: following established form, custom, or rule.

heir apparent: a person who will, without dispute, inherit the property or title of another when that other dies.

hoarded: collected, kept, and stored away.

philosophy: an attitude toward life.

protégé: someone under the guidance of another, especially for her or his career.

Matthew (Matt) Gaines

1. *Flake's Daily Bulletin,* editorial, December 4, 1869.
2. *Ibid.*
3. *Ibid.*
4. Speech, Matthew Gaines, August 10, 1871, as quoted in the *Brenham Banner,* August 15, 1871.
5. *Debates of the Twelfth Legislature.*
6. *Flake's Daily Bulletin,* editorial, December 4, 1869.
7. *Brenham Banner,* September 6, 1871.

accommodations: a place to eat, sleep; traveling space.

African-American: Black American descendant of original Africans; Aframerican.

arrogant: haughty; showing too high an opinion of oneself, or one's position.

auction: a public sale of property; in this case, slaves.

bigamy: illegally having more than one wife or husband at the same time.

bondage: captivity; a state of being bound, usually by law or slavery.

buckboard: a four-wheeled vehicle with a springy platform.

Caucasian: of or relating to the white race of human beings.

characteristics: special qualities that reveal or identify someone or something.

constituents: members of a body of voters.

dignity: the state of being worthy of honor or respect.

dominate: to control; to tower above; to exert authority over.

exiled: banished from one's home or country.

felon: someone guilty of a serious crime; someone guilty of a felony.

freedmen: men freed from slavery.

gesticulations: gestures; movements of the hands or body to express emotion or intention.

harassment: continuous attacks or other unpleasantness.

immigration: the entering of a country or area of which one is not a native to live there permanently.

indicted: formally accused of an offense.

invalid: without foundation in law, truth, or fact.

migrated: moved from one country, place, or locality to another.

mobilize: to put into movement or circulation.

ordained: officially invested as a minister.

ousted: removed from property or position by legal action or force.

paternity: male parentage.

railroaded: pushed through quickly without consideration; convicted in haste with false charges or not enough evidence.

reprimanded: criticized for bad or wrong behavior.

sic: exactly as it is written (to indicate there is no mistake in what has been printed).

subserviently: showing complete submission to another.

urban: of or relating to a city or town.

Barbara Jordan

1. *Austin American-Statesman,* November 23, 1992.

2. *Houston Chronicle,* November 30, 1969.

3. *Ibid.*

4. *Texas Observer,* "A Profile of Barbara Jordan," November 3, 1972.

5. Interview of Dr. Beulah Agnes Curry Jones by the author, April 8, 1995.

6. Barbara Jordan was graduated magna cum laude from Texas Southern University in 1956.

advocate: to urge; to earnestly encourage.

challenge: something which tests a person's qualities.

charismatic: personal leadership magic that wins popular support.

deferred: to postpone; to put off.

emulate: to try to do as well as another.

lottery: a way of raising money by selling many tickets and choosing only a few as winners.

mobility: the state or quality of moving with ease.

orator: a person who speaks in public.

President Pro Tempore: second in command to the president.

George T. "Mickey" Leland

1. *The New York Times Biographical Service,* August 14, 1989.
2. *Ibid.*
3. *THE MAGAZINE* of the *Houston Post,* November 10, 1985.
4. *Ibid.*
5. *Ibid.*
6. *Austin American-Statesman,* August 14, 1989.
7. "Mickey Leland cared deeply about issues he was involved in," by Eddie Reeves, special to the *Austin American–Statesman,* August 1989.

Addis Ababa: capital city of Ethiopia.

Africa: eastern continent, south of Mediterranean.

ambassador: an official of highest rank who represents his or her government in another country.

bigotry: narrow mindedness.

bizarre: strange.

Cuba: Large West Indies island north of Caribbean Sea.

dashiki: a brightly colored loose pullover African shirt, usually with short sleeves.

epitaph: a short, expressive tribute to a dead person, sometimes inscribed on a gravestone.

ethic: system of ethics; relating to morality of behavior.

Ethiopia: Northeast African country south of Egypt, beside Red Sea.

famine: starvation; an extreme lack of food.

frustration: feelings caused when an important need is denied or unsatisfied.

goatee: a small trimmed beard on a man's chin.

hokey: corny; phony; sickly or affectedly sentimental.

Israel: Jewish Mediterranean republic bordering Egypt.

liberal: (politics) favorable to individual liberty, social reform and removal of restraints on production, distribution and consumption of goods and services.

prematurely: occurring before the proper time.

refugee: a person who flees, especially to a foreign country, to escape persecution.

Sudan: a country in northeast Africa south of Egypt.

Talmud: the body of oral Jewish law.

Tanzania: a republic in East Africa.

telecommunication: giving information at a distance by radio, TV, phone, telegraph or cable.

terrain: a stretch of land.

ward: a city division, often for electoral purposes.

Angela Shelf Medearis

chuckling: laughing quietly.
compelling: irresistible, forceful, commanding.
detest: to dislike intensely.
don: to put on.
ecstatic: experiencing extreme joy.
honing: sharpening.
sibling: sister or brother (Medearis has two sisters, and one brother).
vignette: a brief description.

Doris ("Dorie") Miller

1. *Austin American-Statesman,* December 4, 1991
2. *Austin American-Statesman,* August 27, 1990.
3. *Ibid.*
4. *Ibid.*

African-American: Black American descendant of original Africans; Aframerican.
ammunition: everything necessary to feed guns or small arms.
berserk: frenzied; crazed.
D-Day: June 6, 1944, the day Allied forces landed in France in World War II.
decommissioned: retired from active service.
guttural: produced in the throat (harsh, grating, throaty sounds).
masculine: relating to men; characteristic of men.
mess: (military) a number of people, usually of the same rank, who have meals together; the place where they eat; the meals they eat together.
posthumously: after death.
taxidermist: a person who prepares, stuffs, and mounts animal skins.

Bill Pickett

agitated: excited; stirred up.
calving: giving birth to a calf.
dignity: the state of being worthy of honor or respect.
dumbfounded: amazed; astonished.
gore: to pierce or wound with a horn or tusk.
initiate: to get something going; to admit into a special club.
lasso: rope used by a cowboy.
matador: the chief bullfighter.
raucous: behaving in a rough, noisy way.
subdue: to bring under control.
supple: capable of bending easily.
troupe: a group of performers.

Phylicia Rashad

1. *"SISTERS: Debbie Allen and Phylicia Rashad,"* *McCall's* magazine, July 1987.
2. *Ibid.*
3. *Ibid.*
4. *Ibid.*
5. *Ibid.*
6. *Ibid.*
7. *JET* magazine, November 7, 1988.
8. *"SISTERS: Debbie Allen and Phylicia Rashad,"* *McCall's* magazine, July 1987.
9. *Ibid.*
10. *Ibid.*

alma mater: one's school or university.
corrupting: to make wicked.
inherent: belonging by nature; existing in someone or something as a permanent characteristic or quality.
meditation: deep, serious thought.
NBC: National Broadcasting Company.
offhanded: done without preparation.
perspective: evaluation of events according to a particular way of looking at them.
potential: existing but not fully developed; having the capacity to be.
scrape: an awkward or unpleasant situation.
slate: a kind of rock which can be cut and used as a writing surface or roofing tile.
sojourn: to stay or dwell for a time in a place or among certain people.
thronging: crowding together in great numbers.

Ada DeBlanc Simond

1. Robyn Turner, *Austin Originals — Chats with Colorful Characters* (Austin, TX: Paramount Publishing Co., 1982).
2. Interview of Ada Simond by Marian E. Barnes, Austin, January 3, 1986.
3. *Ibid.*
4. Interview of Ada Simond by Marian E. Barnes, Austin, June 20, 1988.
5. Interview of Ada Simond by Marian E. Barnes, Austin, January 3, 1986.
6. Ruthe Winegarten, *Texas Women: A Pictorial History — From Indians to Astronauts,* First Edition (Austin, TX: Eakin Press, 1986), 66.
7. Ada DeBlanc Simond, *Let's Pretend — Mae Dee and Her Family Join the Juneteenth Celebration* (Austin, TX: 1978), ix-x.

8. Funeral service program: *In Loving Memory of Ada Marie DeBlanc Simond,* "Obituary of Ada Marie Simond," Austin, October 26, 1989.

9. *Ibid.*

10. *Ibid.*

catechism: a set of questions and answers on religious doctrine.

catered: provided meals and refreshments.

Creole: a person of African and French or Spanish descent.

eclipsed: diminished the brightness or glory of, especially by excelling.

fictionalized: not restricted to fact.

lucrative: very profitable.

matriculated: to be enrolled in a college or university.

missal: a prayer book.

Mulattos: the children of a Black person and a European.

spinster: an elderly woman who never married.

Heman Marion Sweatt

1. Alwyn Barr, and Robert A. Calvert. *Black Leaders: Texans for Their Times* (Austin, TX: Texas State Historical Association, 1981).

2. *Ibid.*

3. *Ibid.*

4. *Ibid.*

5. *Ibid.*

6. *Ibid.*

accredited: officially authorized or recognized.

audit: to examine or verify (for example, account books).

brief: a concise statement of a client's case to instruct attorneys conducting a law trial.

curriculum: all the courses offered by a school.

devastating: overpowering; overcoming; overwhelming.

extracurricular: student activities officially connected with school, usually having no academic credit.

guinea pig: a person or animal used for experiment.

hamper: to hinder, slow down, or obstruct.

interrogation: the act of questioning.

landmark: an event that marks a turning point.

litigation: the process of taking legal action.

ordeal: an experience that tests character and endurance.

plaintiff: complaining party in a lawsuit to obtain a remedy for an injury to rights.

prestige: respect in the eyes of people.

relentless: mercilessly hard or harsh; the act of someone or something not giving in to appeals or pity.

unanimous: having agreement and consent of all.

Florence Wolfe ("Lady Flo")

adobe: sun-dried brick, not fired in a kiln.
Aframericans: African-Americans.
African-American: an American descendant of original Africans.
bunkhouse: a cabin with narrow sleeping berths for workers on a building site, ranch, etc.
investment: the act of putting money to use to earn a profit.
Los Ojitos: a Spanish term meaning "Little Eyes."
ne'er-do-well: an idle, worthless person.
Negress: a term once used for a female African-American, often considered insulting.
subpoena: a written order commanding a person to appear in a court under penalty.

Marian E. Barnes

1. *Talk That Talk Some More — On the Cutting Room Floor* (Austin, TX: Eakin Press, 1993), 256–355.

African-American: Black American descendant of original Africans; Aframerican.
apex: the highest point.
Caucasian: the white race; of European descent.
caucus: a closed meeting of a group of people belonging to a larger group or political party, to decide policy.
countermand: to revoke a former command by a contrary order.
degrading: lowering in station, rank, or grade.
desperate: having lost hope.
elevating: uplifting; morally, intellectually, or culturally improving.
Great Depression: the period of worldwide economic depression beginning 1929.
Jim Crow laws: legal discrimination against Black Americans.
KKK: Ku Klux Klan, an American secret society founded to maintain white supremacy and oppose Africans and African-Americans, Jews, Catholics, and foreigners; a group with a record of violence against Aframericans.
listless: without energy; uninterested in life.
migration: the act of leaving one country or region to settle in another.
Mrs. Malaprop: a character noted for her humorous misuse of words in *The Rivals*, 1775, a comedy by R. B. Sheridan.
nurture: feed, nourish, sustain, support, keep alive.
NYA: The National Youth Administration was an organization established during the administration of President Franklin Delano Roosevelt. He was assisted by Dr. Mary McLeod Bethune, who was administrator of an Office of Minority Affairs. Later her title was director of the Division of Negro Affairs, and her duties involved granting funds to deserving students, especially African-American students.
unkempt: uncombed, untidy.
unresponsive: not responding, answering, or reacting.

Bibliography

BOOKS

Barnes, Marian E. *Talk That Talk Some More — On the Cutting Room Floor*. Austin, TX: Eakin Press, 1993.

Barr, Alwyn, and Robert A. Calvert. *Black Leaders — Texans for Their Times*. Austin, TX: Texas State Historical Association, 1981.

Biggers, John. *ANANSE — The Web of Life in Africa*. Austin, TX: University of Texas Press, 1962.

Burton, Art. *Black, Red and Deadly*, Austin, TX: Eakin Press, 1991.

Goss, Linda, and Marian E. Barnes. *Talk That Talk — An Anthology of African-American Storytelling*. New York, NY: Simon & Schuster, 1989.

Jordan, Barbara, and Shelby Hearon. *BARBARA JORDAN — Self Portrait*. Garden City, NY: Doubleday & Co., Inc., 1979.

Porter, Eugene O. *Lord Beresford and Lady Flo*. University of Texas at El Paso, 1970.

Rich, Doris L. *Queen Bess — Daredevil Aviator*. Smithsonian Institution Press, 1993.

Simond, Ada DeBlanc. *LET'S PRETEND: Mae Dee and Her Family Go to Town*. Austin, TX: The Stevenson Press, Callcott-Collinson, Inc., 1977.

———. *LET'S PRETEND: Mae Dee and Her Family on a Weekend in May*. Austin, TX: The Stevenson Press, Callcott-Collinson, Inc., 1977.

———. *LET'S PRETEND: Mae Dee and Her Family Join the Juneteenth Celebration*. Austin, TX: The Stevenson Press, Callcott-Collinson, Inc., 1978.

———. *LET'S PRETEND: Mae Dee and Her Family in the Merry, Merry, Season*. Austin, TX: The Stevenson Press, Callcott-Collinson, Inc., 1978.

———. *LET'S PRETEND: Mae Dee and Her Family and the First Wedding of the Year*. Austin, TX: The Stevenson Press, Callcott-Collinson, Inc., 1979.

———. *LET'S PRETEND: Mae Dee and Her Family Ten Years Later*. Austin, TX: The Stevenson Press, Callcott-Collinson, Inc., 1980.

———. *LOOKING BACK*. Austin, TX: Austin Independent School District and The *Austin American-Statesman,* 1983.

Turner, Robyn. *AUSTIN ORIGINALS — Chats With Colorful Characters*. Amarillo, TX: Paramount Publishing Co., 1982.

Wilson, Merzie. *BESSIE COLEMAN, Merzette Black History Coloring Book*. Merzie Wilson, 4221 Otter Street, Philadelphia, PA, 1990.

CONSULTATIONS

Jones, Dr. Beulah Agnes Curry Chairwoman, Dept. of Music, Huston-Tillotson College, Austin. Re: *DR. VIRGIE CARRINGTON DEWITTY and THREE DIVAS ON STAGE;* intermittent dates during March and April of 1995.

Kimbrough, Dr. Marvin, Chairperson, Division of Humanities, Huston-Tillotson College. Re: *ADA DeBLANC SIMOND*, April 24, 1995.

Mays, Ms. Martha, DeWitty family historian. Re: *DR. VIRGIE CARRINGTON DEWITTY,* April 23, 1995.

Sawyer, Cheryl Delco. Communications Mgr., The ARC of Texas, Austin. Re: *WILHELMINA RUTH FITZGERALD DELCO,* February 28, 1995.

FUNERAL SERVICE PROGRAM

In Loving Memory of Ada Marie DeBlanc Simond. Holy Cross Catholic Church, Austin, Texas, October 26, 1989.

INTERVIEWS

Delco, Wilhelmina Fitzgerald, by Marian E. Barnes, Austin, Texas, February 24, 1995.

Jones, Dr. Beulah Agnes, by Marian E. Barnes, Austin, Texas, April 14, 1995.

Medearis, Angela Shelf, by Marian E. Barnes, Austin, Texas, 1994.

Simond, Ada DeBlanc, by Marian E. Barnes, Austin, Texas, January 3, 1986, and June 20, 1988.

MAGAZINES

Brooks, Alberta. Edited by General Berry, Jr. *"No More House Work." OUR TEXAS,* Winter 1995.

Flatow, Sheryl. "SISTERS: Debbie Allen and Phylicia Rashad." *McCall's,* July, 1987.

The Magazine of The Houston Post, November 10, 1983.

MONOGRAPHS

Southwestern Studies, Monograph No. 25. Porter, Eugene O. "Lord Beresford & Lady Flo," University of Texas at El Paso, 1970.

NEWSPAPERS

Austin American-Statesman. April 15, 1993. "Tutors Page for Reading."
———. June 12, 1992. "Unity Day to Celebrate Racial Harmony."
———. July 23, 1992. John Bryant, "Brains Toned With Zavala Reading Program."
———. December 4, 1991. "Waco Man Rose from Dining Helper to Hero During Pearl Harbor Attack."
———. October 23, 1989. Meredith McKittrick, "Black Writer Ada Simond Dies at 85."

————. August 14, 1989. "Leland's Plane Found Destroyed."

————. August 12, 1980. "Friends Mourn DeWitty With her Own Songs."

Dallas Morning News. July 1, 1973. "Destroyer Escort Named for Texan."

The New York Times Biographical Service, August 1989, "Representative Mickey Leland, 44, Dies in Crash."

The Villager. October 27, 1989. Dorothey Charles Banks, "Local Writer, Historian, Ada Simond Leaves Mark on Austin."

REFERENCE WORKS

Adams, Russell L. *Great Negroes Past and Present.* 3rd ed. Chicago: Afro-Am Publishing Co., 1984.

Brown, John E., and Roger P. Nelson. *AFRO USA — A Reference Work on the Black Experience.* New York: Bellwether Publishing Co., 1971.

Moritz, Charles. *Current Biography Yearbook 1987.* "Debbie Allen." New York: H. W. Wilson, Co., 1987.